Godman to Tycoon

Godman to Tycoon

The Untold Story of Baba Ramdev

Priyanka Pathak-Narain

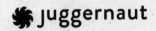

JUGGERNAUT BOOKS
KS House, 118 Shahpur Jat, New Delhi 110049, India

First published by Juggernaut Books 2017

Copyright © Priyanka Pathak-Narain 2017

10 9 8 7 6 5 4 3 2 1

All rights reserved. No part of this publication may be reproduced, transmitted, or stored in a retrieval system in any form or by any means without the written permission of the publisher.

The views and opinions expressed in this book are the author's own. The facts contained herein were reported to be true as on the date of publication by the author to the publishers of the book, and the publishers are not in any way liable for their accuracy or veracity.

ISBN 9789386228383

Typeset in Adobe Caslon Pro by R. Ajith Kumar, New Delhi

Printed at Manipal Technologies Ltd

Contents

Author's Note vii

1. The Tycoon — 1
2. The Boy Ramdev — 13
3. The Deputy and the Mentor — 25
4. The Guru — 33
5. The Early Days — 41
6. Aastha Television — 49
7. The TV Star — 53
8. Friends in High Places — 63
9. Mystery 1: The Ally's Murder — 69
10. A New Mentor Enters — 71
11. The Old Mentor Exits — 75
12. The Seeds of an Empire — 81
13. Enter Brinda Karat — 89
14. Patanjali Is Born — 97
15. The Yoga Roadshow — 99
16. Mystery 2: The Guru's Disappearance — 105

Contents

17.	The Reinvention	115
18.	The Aastha Takeover	121
19.	Mystery 3: The Mentor's Sudden Death	129
20.	The Anna Movement	143
21.	The Old Mentor Re-enters	153
22.	The CEO	159
23.	The Brother	183
24.	Patanjali Ayurveda Limited	189
25.	Conclusion	201

Sources	209
Acknowledgements	235
A Note on the Author	237

Author's Note

When the idea for a book on Baba Ramdev and his company came up, it seemed promising. I had followed Ramdev's rise ten years ago when I was at *Mint*, meeting him on multiple occasions, covering his Ganga campaign in Kanpur, hanging around his kutir while he asked questions about swadeshi economics to Rajeev Dixit, his late mentor. I enjoyed listening to their easy banter and all the idealism in their conversation at the time.

Each time we met, I had found him earthy, self-deprecating and disarming, generous with his time and deft in steering conversations to what he wanted to say. But I never felt that I had really got to know him. Beyond his carefully cultivated public persona lay a masterfully guarded person of tremendous will.

The only way to tell his story, I believed, was to tell it through the voices of all the people he worked with

Author's Note

along the way to building his empire, those who'd had a chance to meet him in unguarded moments. I imagined that their memories, anecdotes, tales of how Ramdev inspired and transformed their lives would be a far more interesting story than Ramdev's own version of it.

So I began at the beginning. I spoke to members of Ramdev's family: from his mother, Gulabo Devi, and brother Devdutt Yadav to his uncle Jagdeesh Yadav. They gave me a rare glimpse into Ramdev's childhood and adolescent years. I spoke to his friends: from his junior at the gurukul he attended in his early twenties, Acharya Abhaydev, who shared anecdotes about Ramdev's tenacity, to his lifelong deputy, Acharya Balkrishna. I interviewed long-time Haridwar residents Sushant Mahendru and Tarun Kumar, who have known Ramdev and company since their early days selling chawanprash on bicycles there. I spoke to Radhika Nagrath, who helped design Ramdev's first logo, and to Professor Veena Shastri, another Haridwar old-timer, who has witnessed at close quarters Ramdev's phenomenal rise and remembers, for instance, the old days when Ramdev's brother used to go on a cycle to deliver fresh milk to his sister in the hostel where she stayed in Haridwar. I spoke at length to his first mentor, Karamveer Maharaj, with whom Ramdev later fell out, and, when he was still alive, to his second mentor, Rajeev Dixit, the architect

Author's Note

of Ramdev's swadeshi campaign. I met people who had worked for Ramdev at different points of time – from Vipin Pradhan, an aide of Ramdev's between 2002 and 2005, before Patanjali Ayurveda Ltd was even established, to S.K. Patra, the CEO who helped lay the foundations for Patanjali's phenomenal growth. I hunted down Kirit Mehta, a bitter former ally of Ramdev's, and one of the founders of Aastha TV; and the Pitties, still devoted Ramdev supporters. I interviewed Ramdev's adversaries and officers investigating him and his firms for various alleged lapses – from Brinda Karat, who levelled the sensational charge that Ramdev's Ayurvedic medicines contained unlabelled human and animal bones, to Jitendar Rana, who investigated Ramdev for sales tax evasion. All in all, I spoke to fifty-two people to unravel the mystery. My sources corroborated – and dismissed – information that I had gathered from other primary sources, helping me fill in the gaps until a clear narrative began to emerge.

Some of my interlocuters – Karamveer, Kirit Mehta and S.K. Patra, for instance – are important new voices in the Ramdev story, who agreed to taped interviews and spoke for the first time on the record about their time with Ramdev. For a complete list of inverviewees and sources for each chapter, please refer to 'Sources' at the end of the book.

Author's Note

I had set off expecting to discover a rags-to-riches tale, of how a boy with no formal education became a national hero and tycoon through sheer grit, determination, hard work and conviction. I did find a portion of that story. But I also found much more.

1

The Tycoon

Haridwar, 2016

On a low stage, sunlight streaming from a high skylight, he lies flat on his stomach, props a shaggy face on his palms, peers into the crowd and laughs. A thousand people mimic his yogic pose and laugh back indulgently.

There never was any doubt about this nimble, orange-robed man's ability to grip an audience. He has held millions enthralled, day after day, for more than a decade. Like any good performer, Baba Ramdev knows the trick is to keep surprising.

So, sitting beside towers of products made by his company, Patanjali Ayurveda, during one of his telecast yoga camps, this improbable business tycoon with an eye for drama smiles and says, 'Patanjali has become a great brand, I hear. But you've seen nothing yet. There are two things that I have to do. Make all foreign companies do sirshasana [headstand] within five years, and put Mother India on the throne of the world. *Kitna maza ayega* [What fun it'll be]!'

Cheers and enthusiastic applause greet the announcement. He holds everyone spellbound in his theatre – some are smitten, others cynical, but hardly any are indifferent. How can they be? Baba Ramdev's story and his rise are simply stunning.

Born Ram Kisan Yadav, the ill-educated son of an impoverished farmer from Said Alipur, Haryana, Ramdev began his tenuous journey to fame and fortune as a yoga teacher struggling to help his family make ends meet sometime in the late 1980s. Three decades later, Baba Ramdev is the powerful tycoon at the helm of Patanjali Ayurveda Limited, the country's fastest-growing FMCG, or 'fast moving consumer goods', company that employs about 20,000 people.

If the big three FMCG companies, Unilever, Colgate and Nestlé, are worried and frequently looking over their shoulder, it's for good reason.

Revenues at Patanjali Ayurveda multiplied fifteen times from Rs 317 crore at the end of 2010–11 to an awe-inspiring Rs 5000 crore in 2015–16. Ramdev declared that this number would double by the end of 2016–17. It did – to a staggering Rs 10,000 crore in May 2017. While announcing this stupendous achievement,

Ramdev set the company's next audacious target: Rs 20,000 crore in revenue by May 2018.

A 2017 Assocham-TechSci research report put this growth in perspective thus: Patanjali is 'the most disruptive force in the Indian FMCG market'. While Patanjali is growing at over 100 per cent annually, 'its peers including ITC, Dabur, Hindustan Unilever [HUL], Colgate–Palmolive and Procter & Gamble struggled to get a growth much less than double digit'.

In September 2016 the Hurun Rich List, a ranking of dollar billionaires in the world, listed Baba Ramdev's closest aide, Acharya Balkrishna, as the twenty-sixth richest Indian, with a personal wealth of Rs 25,600 crore ($3.8 billion). He owns 94 per cent of Patanjali Ayurveda Ltd. Swamis, such as Baba Ramdev, who have taken sanyas and wear saffron clothes as a mark of their renunciation of the pursuit of worldly things like wealth and fame and forsaken their families are prohibited by the code of ascetics from owning companies. If Baba Ramdev accepted a direct stake in Patanjali Ayurveda, he would violate that sacrosanct code of religious ethics and lose credibility with his followers. That's why Balkrishna, the deputy whom Ramdev keeps on a tight leash, is Patanjali Ayurveda's primary shareholder.

When you first meet Ramdev one of the first things you notice is his flowing hair and beard, lightly shot with silver. In keeping with the tenets of sanyasis, he wears a uniform of a saffron dhoti and uses another unstitched piece of saffron cloth to cover his upper body, like one would with a shawl. Ramdev's skin glows and he seems like a beacon of good health. He's constantly smiling and cheerful, and is a fast and energetic talker. Ramdev always strives to put the person at the other end of the table at ease, he wants you to like him, and will put up a little show full of humour, bombast and coyness to reel in his audience. He shares his grand vision and grander plans, and it is hard not to smile back and like this beaming man. Ever the adept conversationalist, Ramdev can skilfully steer conversation to where he wants it to go. At the end of an hours-long meeting with him, you first feel warm and fuzzy, but then you may feel that you've been outwitted, that you know nothing at all about Ramdev.

When Balkrishna is in Ramdev's presence, this short, stocky man with a boyish face, always dressed in white, stays quiet. He respectfully cedes the stage to Ramdev. On the whole, Balkrishna, who, like Ramdev, has glowing skin, seems less confident and more tentative than his boss. He, too, is desperate to be liked but isn't as outgoing or energetic as Ramdev. When you meet Balkrishna one on one, he is haughty and a bit cagey. Not as worldly-wise as Ramdev, Balkrishna can fly into a temper and even yell at you for asking 'inappropriate' questions – something the cautious Ramdev would never do. Balkrishna is a hard-working deputy and looks up to Baba Ramdev. Slightly insecure, he seems to covet Ramdev's fame and stature. Perhaps that's why he's so active on social media, building up his own presence. And maybe it is Balkrishna who's responsible for the gradual change in the culture of Ramdev's empire: people who work there always used to touch Ramdev's feet but now they touch Balkrishna's too.

But do not mistake Ramdev for just another saffron-robed sanyasi, warns S.K. Patra, former CEO of Patanjali Ayurveda and president of Patanjali Food Park from 2011 to 2014, and architect of the company's astonishing growth. 'He has a prodigious imagination and terrific business sense. He may have a squint eye, but he knows where the money is.'

Offering over 500 FMCG products ranging from creams, shampoos and household cleaners to biscuits and clarified butter, Baba Ramdev has found a wide consumer base at the bottom of the pyramid that other companies had not even noticed, let alone made an effort to cater to. His products, made from natural ingredients, including soap made from cow dung and floor cleaners made from cow urine, have expanded and deepened the market and brought a new consuming class from the fringes into the marketplace. Nearly 56 per cent of his company's revenues come from the food and health-care sectors. The rest come from toiletries, dental and hair products, and cosmetics.

An outspoken critic of western capitalism, Ramdev sees his competitors as mortal enemies and invites his followers to do so too. During televised yoga lessons on the television network that he owns, he deftly adds a twist of fear-mongering among India's newly minted consuming classes that believe him to be a godman: the products made by competing foreign companies are 'slow poison', he says.

Embracing protectionist rhetoric in a global economy, he compares foreign companies presently working and generating jobs in India to the East India Company, the English company that established the British Raj in India that would continue for two centuries. 'They take away millions of dollars from the country in profits ... they are looting our nation,' he alleges energetically.

In a country whose freedom struggle was underpinned by Gandhi's 'swadeshi' movement, where the word 'swadeshi' evokes emotional memories of British domination – images of destroyed local industry, of craftsmen whose hands were cut off, of people carrying British-made goods out of their homes and tossing them on to huge burning pyres – Ramdev cleverly crafts his rhetoric to yoke his commerce to a lofty and noble ideal.

Although it is believed that Ramdev enjoys the

support and encouragement of the current government in his drive to expand his empire, it is also true that his economic agenda does not align with the economic agenda of Narendra Modi's administration. While the prime minister has travelled to over thirty countries to drum up international interest in his Make in India campaign to induce foreign investors to manufacture here, Ramdev enjoys shocking people by threatening to drive foreign investors out.

'*Colgate ka gate bhi band hoga, Pantene ka to pant gila hone wala hai, Unilever ka lever bhi baithega aur Nestlé ki chidiya bhi udegi.* [The "gate" of Colgate will shut, Pantene will wet its pants, the lever of Unilever will break down, and the little Nestlé bird will fly away],' Ramdev said in 2016, declaring war on the country's three largest FMCG multinationals whose combined revenue is nearly nine times his own.

But these companies have remained stoic amid Ramdev's relentless attacks. A senior executive at one of these companies, on the condition of anonymity, said, 'We have been here for a century and will be here for another one. We are as Indian as anyone else. His company has shown that there is untapped market potential and we see that. Why engage in a verbal war with anyone? Let actions speak.'

Well, their actions are speaking: Hindustan Unilever and Colgate have learned from Ramdev and have begun injecting their product ranges with a herbal and Ayurvedic dose. For instance, HUL bought over Indulekha, an Ayurvedic hair oil company, in 2015 and will once again compete in the hair oil category that it had left ten years ago when it sold Nihar, its coconut oil brand, to Marico. L'Oreal, the French cosmetics firm, is researching on Ayurvedic herbs in a laboratory in south India. In August 2016, in a direct challenge to Patanjali Ayurveda, Colgate–Palmolive launched a brand-new 'natural' toothpaste, made with lemon, cloves and salt, and with a truly Indian name: Vedshakti. In April 2017 Dabur announced the launch of Ask Dabur, a call centre where doctors will advise callers on Ayurveda and help consumers sift through a bewildering array of 'natural' and 'herbal' products and medicines.

In ways that he may not have foreseen himself, Ramdev has managed to make the world sit up and take note of yoga and Ayurveda and may well have changed the market forever in India.

Yet, the battle has only just begun. Baba Ramdev, while forcing global giants to follow his lead, has set an even more audacious target for 2019–20: to multiply Patanjali's revenue to Rs 50,000 crore by that year's end. If he manages that, he would have outstripped all three conglomerates put together. In May 2016, stroking his wiry, untamed beard, he said mysteriously, 'I have plans.'

It was easy to believe that – the surprises have already begun.

In August 2016 Baba Ramdev birthed another brand, Astha, under the Patanjali umbrella to compete in the Rs 8000 crore category of home worship products. Sold online on Shubhkart.com, Astha has hundreds of products, belonging to eighteen different categories, including Indian clothing, idols for worship at home, Vaastu and fengshui products, shaligram (holy stones), rudraksha (holy beads) and even fresh packaged prasad shipped from a dozen popular temples around the country.

The very next month, in September 2016, Baba Ramdev was on stage again unveiling 'swadeshi' jeans for Indian women – loose-fitting pants that cover up curves in a culturally appropriate manner. Balkrishna, who is gradually emerging from Ramdev's shadow, said in an interview to the *Economic Times*, 'We got this idea to manufacture swadeshi jeans because every year there is a lot that Indians spend on buying jeans that largely come from big companies. We want to make sure all the jeans we wear are home-made.'

Within two months, Baba Ramdev's Patanjali Ayurveda had entered two new categories – apparel and home worship. There is no telling what he might do next, or which sector he might decide to enter with a slew of new products.

'With Baba Ramdev, all bets are off,' says Aditya Pittie, son of an old partner and disciple, who holds exclusive distribution rights for Patanjali Ayurveda products in Mumbai. The Pitties are also Patanjali's exclusive distributors to organized retail stores and have global distribution rights in the home worship category. 'He takes very quick decisions and is never hung up about what he had said he would or would not do. Look at noodles. He had said he would never sell them. He rolled them out in three months' time [by November 2015, when Nestlé's Maggi noodles was embroiled in a controversy and was banned for a while by India's food safety authorities]. He will do whatever is needed for the good of the people and the country.'

Pittie is right. Baba Ramdev has never felt encumbered by what he may have said in the past – and while the spiritual world may frown upon such rapid changes of stance, adaptability is not a bad thing in the real world of business. At one time, Baba Ramdev was adamant that advertising was a waste of money. It is easy to see why he had thought this: he owns Aastha and Sanskar, the two largest religious television networks in the country. So why would he want to pay for product exposure?

But then, by November 2015, he changed his mind. Soon after Patanjali launched noodles, Ramdev began spending on traditional advertising in a big way. For nine of the following twelve weeks, Patanjali topped the weekly list of total ad insertions, according to the television viewership measurement agency Broadcast Audience Research Council (BARC) India. Its weekly television ads more than doubled from 11,897 in the first week of January 2016 to 24,050 in the week ended 25 March. During the same period, Ramdev appeared 2,34,934 times across TV channels, which means he was on air every 30 seconds on one channel or another. He never looked back. A year later, in the week beginning 6 May 2017 and ending 12 May, Patanjali Ayurveda Limited remained among the top ten advertisers in India.

Each of these advertisements prominently features a beaming Baba Ramdev, and, of late, Balkrishna too. Other than Lee Iacocca for Ford, Steve Jobs for Apple and Bill Gates for Microsoft, there are very few examples of proprietors or CEOs becoming successful brand ambassadors for their companies. There were none in India. Until Baba Ramdev became the face of Patanjali Ayurveda.

Questioned during a television interview if a sanyasi should be running a business empire, Baba Ramdev responded, in his trademark style, with a faux aggressive counter-question, smile on his face. 'Accha,' he demanded, tilting his head in that familiar way, 'show me where in our scriptures is it written that a sanyasi has to retire to the Himalayas and do nothing else? I am a karma yogi and a rashtra yogi . . . The purpose is not to accumulate any great wealth for myself. Look, there is an empire worth crores, no, hundreds of crores around us today [referring to Patanjali's assets], but even today, I sleep in a hut on the floor. Whatever I have got from the country, it is for the country. The wealth of Patanjali is not for any one person – it is for the country. It is all for charity.'

It is difficult not to admire the sentiment. Or the devotion with which he set off to bring yoga and Ayurveda to millions of Indians – not the kind that live in Delhi and Mumbai alone but also the ones who live in Tier 2 and 3 cities. Baba Ramdev kindled the resurgence of yoga in the country at the turn of the millennium when he would appear on television every morning to teach yoga in his homely and practical way.

Yet, after fifteen years of seeing him on television networks, at the helm of a national anti-corruption movement that threatened to topple the United Progressive Alliance (UPA) 2 government and, of late, in newspaper ads and on billboards, questions about him stubbornly linger: Who is Baba Ramdev? Where did he come from? How did he go from contorting his body into yogic poses on television to creating India's fastest-growing FMCG companies? Are his products really as good as he claims they are? Is he a visionary? Is he a fraud? What drives him?

2

The Boy Ramdev

Said Alipur, 1965–75

Said Alipur, Haryana, is a bleak place.

The village itself is a huddle of ill-kept mud and stone houses surrounded by brown fields and an arid, treeless country. Here, the earth has to be coaxed, wheedled into birthing. For the farmers, a bad monsoon determines their precarious fate – life or death.

In the receding light of day, returning camel carts knock about its tortuous alleys, so roiled by the elements that they look like craters on the moon. After dark, the women withdraw behind doors. Youths with powerful shoulders emerge from the shadows of lantern lights and join the men drawing deeply on hookahs with glowing embers.

A few decades ago, sometime in the years between

1965 and 1975, a fierce farmer named Ram Nivas Yadav sat among them. For a month, his wife, Gulabo Devi, lay in a tiny, windowless chamber – awaiting the birth to their second child.

When he came, they named the boy Ram Kisan.

Ram Kisan Yadav, later Baba Ramdev, is reluctant to share the date or year of his birth. Various birthdates are mentioned on unofficial websites – 25 December 1965, January 1968 and even as late as December 1975 – but none are verifiable.

To these and many other questions about their past during an interview, Ramdev and Balkrishna responded by repeatedly telling me to look for the answers in an 'official' biography, written in Hindi, titled *Swami Ramdev: Ek Yogi, Ek Yodhha*, by the journalist Sandeep Dev. Balkrishna helpfully gave me a copy during the interview.

Sandeep Dev recounts the struggle to get Ramdev to answer the question about his date of birth: 'I begged him to tell me his birthdate, nearly fell at his feet, but he only smiled at me and said, "I really was born only on April 9, 1995, the day my guru, Shankar Devji Maharaj, gave me sanyas deeksha [that is, the day Ramdev donned his saffron robes and renounced the world]. So it is better to keep that only as my birthdate."'

A search at the public records room at the civil hospital in Narnaul (where birth and death records for

Said Alipur are kept) yielded nothing. 'He was born at home. Maybe his parents never bothered registering his birth? It was not uncommon all those years ago. Record-keeping was not as good as it is today,' said Mohit Soni, clerk in the small record room, as we pored over names of babies from Said Alipur village born in the years suspected to be the birth years of Baba Ramdev.

~

Said Alipur is a part of Mahendragarh district, one of the most backward in the country even today, according to the ministry of panchayati raj, which included it in the Backward Regions Grant Fund Scheme.

While the national sex ratio in 2011 was 919 women for every 1000 men, the sex ratio in Mahendragarh was 877, down from 918 in 2001. It was even worse in the 0–6 age group, where it fell from 818 in 2001 to 778 in 2011. Such sharp declines are considered by experts to be a clear indication of sex selection and female foeticide and infanticide. Haryana is also a state with very low groundwater reserves and the number of farmer suicides here was five times that in the neighbouring states of Himachal Pradesh and Punjab in 2014 alone.

By all accounts, conditions in Said Alipur were similar in the decade of Ramdev's birth. After Ramdev was born, two more children – a boy and a girl – were born to his parents, who did not have the resources to raise four children. The children slept on the floor and played with a ball made of tightly rolled-up rags. Still, three boys were a welcome addition to a farming household – sturdy farmhands to help their father put food on the table.

Except that Ramdev was not a strong boy. Rather, he was a sickly, accident-prone child who very nearly died several times in his infancy and childhood. 'Had it not been for the diligent care of my mausi [mother's sister] and my mother, I probably would have,' he says.

According to some accounts, soon after he was born, it was noticed that something was wrong with the baby's face. A paralysis set in at infancy that permanently damaged his face and left him with a twitching eye.

His mother discreetly went to a doctor in the nearby town to get her son some medical attention, any medicine that could help her boy. Discretion was paramount because she did not want her mother-in-law to know that she had sought a doctor's aid. 'My grandmother believed the paralysis was the result of the wrath of a goddess. When my mother returned with the medicine, my grandmother forced her to throw it out,' remembers his older brother, Devdutt Yadav, standing in the desolate courtyard of their childhood home. 'So he was given no treatment and my mother had to watch as the paralysis claimed half his face.'

The Boy Ramdev

This was just one of a series of afflictions and accidents that marked young Ramdev's childhood. When he was two, he leaned far over the edge of a high rafter in his house to watch his aunt working below. 'I toppled, head first, on to the ground. It was a miracle that I survived with just this mark,' he says, pointing to a deep scar on his forehead. Ramdev's official biography makes no mention of this incident, but in the official documentary about his life, *Yog Yatra*, the accident is said to have happened while he was playing with his sister.

Not long after he took this tumble, Ramdev nearly drowned in the village temple's pond while playing with some boys. If a passer-by had not dived in to rescue him, it is said, he may have died.

During his early childhood Ramdev also became so obese 'that I had to be carried about. I had massive, painful boils on my legs,' he says, cupping his hands to demonstrate their golf-ball size. 'I still have marks on my thighs.'

But born into a poor farming family and with a rather hard man for a father, Ramdev was not let off the heavy farm work because of his infirmities. As part of his chores, he had to till the land, care for the farm animals and carry heavy pans of cow dung on his head. This apparently deformed his skull – a disfigurement, he asserts, the practice of yoga eventually fixed.

So Ramdev had a partially paralysed face, he was

unusually fat and accident- and illness-prone – it is not surprising then that he preferred his own company as a child. People from his school and village remember teasing him. He was called Kaniya, a derogatory term for squint-eye, which hurt him as a boy.

When Ramdev got into middle school, he had to walk a couple of kilometres to the village school in Shabajpur, in unstable slippers made of tyres, and with second-hand books and a scrap of jute to sit on. The school was in a ramshackle building with doors that swung on broken hinges and classrooms that doubled up as a shelter for stray animals at night.

It was not an easy life for anyone in the village of Said Alipur. While Ramdev's family struggled and survived, many others didn't. Farmer suicides were common then too, and according to his family, they distressed Ramdev very much. 'He used to cry and demand to know why the government did nothing to help us,' his father recalled.

Ramdev's father was not just a tough taskmaster. He was also given to bouts of rage that marred Ramdev's childhood. When Ramdev was about fifteen years old, some supplies were found missing from the school kitchen. A few boys had stolen oil to make pakoras. When the theft was noticed, the boys blamed it on Ramdev.

According to some accounts, Ramdev's father was furious on hearing the allegation. He did not stop to ask his son for an explanation. He simply tied Ramdev's arms, strung him up from a ceiling beam and began beating him mercilessly with a massive stump of wood. Ramdev recalled, 'I kept screaming and shouting that I had not stolen anything. My mother was crying, but nothing affected him. He told my mother that if she tried to protect me, he would hit her too. My poor mother kept crying. He only stopped when he was so exhausted that he could hit me no more ... after a few days, the real culprits were caught. But it made no impact on my father. He did not seem to realize that he had hit me without cause. In fact, it seemed as though it made no difference to him at all.'

Old neighbours remember this was not an unusual event. Ram Nivas Yadav often beat his children for transgressions – real and imagined.

Hemmed in by desperate poverty, a violent home in an unfriendly village, and reeling under financial difficulties and caste prejudices, Ramdev was bright enough to see what the rest of his life would be like if he stayed in the village: marriage would swiftly follow an inadequate education, more years of sleeping on the floor of the same low mud house, fighting his brothers for his portion of their father's land to eke out whatever meagre existence he could for himself and his family. All this would unfold in the eternal shadow of debt.

This was not a life he could accept.

He says he found himself drawn to wandering Arya Samaj pracharaks, who seemed calmer and more purposeful than anyone else he had met. The Arya Samaj, started by Swami Dayanand Saraswati in 1875, is a Hindu reformist movement. Its proponents opposed the caste system, idol worship and elaborate rituals, but taught yoga and the Vedas. Its missionaries travelled from village to village, mobilizing support for its nationalist and religious initiatives.

An impressionable Ramdev took refuge in their books and their tales of men who rose to greatness against insurmountable odds, perhaps seeing some of his own struggles in their stories. 'A brahmachari lent me a book on Dayanand Saraswatiji's life . . . it influenced me. I realized western education was not true to the heritage of India, that it was meant to enslave our minds into thinking all western things are better than our own,' remembers Ramdev. 'He was a great promoter of gurukuls and I was very inspired by his life.'

The teenaged Ramdev began to see a way out for himself – run away from home. Was it the material and intellectual poverty or the violence of his home that drove him away? Or was he, as he claims, running towards the ambition to stand on the grand stage of nation-building? Or was it a bit of this and that? It is impossible to know.

So one fine morning, he left. And here, obfuscation

flirts with craftsmanship, again, for there are two competing narratives to this tale.

The first is Ramdev's own version that he refuses to talk about now. He directs you to his biography where the story goes as follows: On the morning of 4 October, when he was sixteen, Ramdev stole out of the house while his family slept. He wore khaki trousers and a blue shirt. An unnamed friend bore him away on a cycle to the nearest bus stop, of Nangal Chaudhry, about six kilometres away. Ramdev recollects the day, the month, his age and what clothes he wore, but like all key life events before 1995, he is not keen on sharing the year. He says he does not remember it. Ramdev's biography goes on to enumerate the struggle, hunger and hardship he encountered during his lonely search for a gurukul, a residential school that teaches disciples Sanskrit and Hindu scriptures, across northern India.

However, his uncle Jagdeesh Yadav, who was a part of the joint family and still lives in Said Alipur, tells a different story. Jagdeesh Yadav said that on a summer morning in 1988, about a year after they had installed a tube well in their fields, after a scolding from his father, 'Ram Kisan came running to me because he wanted to go away. I took him to the gurukul at Khanpur, 30 kilometres away.' If Ramdev was born in 1965 or 1968, as some suspect he was, he would have been in his early twenties.

One way or another, Ramdev found himself at the doorstep of Khanpur gurukul, an educational institution that awarded no degrees, 30 kilometres from his home. The Vedic gurukul system of education, where students live in the establishment of their teacher, was said to be the primary educational institution in India before British rule. Students from all classes of society would live with their teacher, learning from him and also helping him with household chores.

Acharya Abhaydev, the current headmaster of the institution, remembers the boy Ramdev vividly. When I went to meet him, the sun was slipping behind the single-storey school building that rose amid flat, brown fields. Parrots chirped in trees above and cows lowed in their stalls. 'Ramdev was my senior when I came here,' says Abhaydev, sitting in the courtyard of the school that Ramdev had once studied in, slept in and often cleaned.

'The boys used to tease him about his squint eye . . . but he was an angry, determined young man. Once our teacher wanted to make a toilet in his room for his personal use. When some boys laughed at Ramdev's offer to help, he dug a fifty-foot pit all by himself, almost with his bare hands,' recollects Abhaydev, still marvelling at his stubborn determination. 'He took a bucket, tied it to a rope. Then he tied the rope to a pole. He'd fill up the bucket with earth, climb up to the top of the pit using the rope, pull the bucket out behind him and toss out the dirt. Then he'd throw the bucket back in, slither back down into the pit, and start filling up the bucket all over again.'

From there, Ramdev proceeded to gurukul Kalwa, another institution of learning that didn't award formal degrees and that, like the Khanpur gurukul, was not recognized by the government. These were the places where he learned Sanskrit grammar, tended cows, collected alms from the nearby villages, performed headstands and other complex yogic kriyas, or breathing exercises and postures.

This was also where Ramdev formed a friendship with his future deputy-to-be, Acharya Balkrishna.

3

The Deputy and the Mentor

Haridwar, early 1992

Acharya Balkrishna, a young man with a high-pitched voice and protruding teeth, was born Balkrishna Suvedi. Still a few months shy of his twentieth birthday, Balkrishna was Ramdev's junior at Gurukul Kalwa and used to occasionally learn Sanskrit grammar from him. The gurukul was a harsh place, full of hardships, and Balkrishna's heart was in the countryside, in the forests and mountains. So every now and then, when the rigour and discipline of gurukul life became too much to bear, Balkrishna set off on his own. Between the late 1980s and early 1990s he often left his gurukuls to wander the country learning Ayurveda from Ayurvedic doctors, or vaidyas, by serving as their assistant.

Little is known about Balkrishna. Although it is

claimed that he was born in Kankhal, Haridwar, no one can say for certain whether he was indeed born there, or in Nepal, as is widely believed. In 2011 the Central Bureau of Investigation alleged that he had submitted fake educational degrees to the government in 2005 in order to procure an Indian passport. That case is still ongoing.

On this particular interlude from gurukul life, he had gone to Kankhal in Haridwar, where his father had worked as a guard and he'd lived as an infant with six brothers, with a goal: he wanted to reach Gaumukh, the glacier where the Ganga is born. But his timing was wrong: the caverns of the Gangotri that birthed the Ganga were deep-frozen spaces at that time of year. Passage was impossible. Even the Gangotri temple, dedicated to the river, was closed through the winter. As Balkrishna walked along the canal fed by the Ganga in Haridwar, looking lost and seeking someone to give him direction, a man called Karamveer noticed him.

'I was cycling to my university from the ashram where I was living at the time, when I first noticed an earnest young man in white clothes and large wooden sandals too big for him,' recalls Karamveer. 'Very nice kid, I'd thought to myself. But I was late for class and had no time to stop.' So Karamveer cycled on, unaware that he'd just seen one of his two future partners, a stone's throw from an ashram they were destined to inherit.

The Deputy and the Mentor

Destiny wasted no time – that very evening, it contrived a meeting between the two future partners of Patanjali at an ashram called Patanjali Yog Dham.

Karamveer often called on a swami there. 'When I went after college . . . [I] found Balkrishna sitting with him, stubbornly insisting that he wanted to go to Gangotri.' Finally, fed up with Balkrishna's obstinacy, the swami passed him on to Karamveer. 'He's been going for fifteen years. Why don't you talk to him?'

Delighted, Balkrishna turned his attention to Karamveer. 'I told him he simply could not go, all roads are snowed under and it is very cold . . . But that I would be going there in the summer again. I said, "If you like, you can come with me this year."'

Thus, an unlikely friendship sprung up between Karamveer and Balkrishna – an erudite academic from one of India's premier traditional universities and the earnest boy with a middling education from an unrecognized, no-name gurukul in the backwaters of Haryana.

~

Karamveer's story is important because he was instrumental in giving Ramdev and Balkrishna the leg-up they needed to become who they are today.

A stoic, soft-spoken sanyasi with startling blue eyes,

Karamveer thinks deeply before he speaks. He has a certain gravitas, a self-assuredness that makes it apparent that he does not care if his audience likes him or not. Family, friends, acquaintances and teachers corroborate all the key facts of his life.

Like Ramdev, Karamveer too does not reveal his birth year. Like Ramdev, he grew up in a tiny village, Titoda in Uttar Pradesh. Like Ramdev, he found himself drawn to the teachings of the Arya Samaj. And like Ramdev, he was also a bit of a loner.

But the similarity ends there.

Karamveer's family was better off. His father, also a farmer, supplemented his income with a transport business. He'd hoped his son Karamveer would inherit it some day, not knowing that a householder's life did not appeal to his son. Karamveer attended school, and went to college in the mid 1980s. His heart was in studying ancient Indian texts so he studied Sanskrit at Meerut University and by 1988 he had arrived in Haridwar where he would pursue three postgraduate degrees in yoga, Indian philosophy and the Vedas from Gurukul Kangri Vishwavidyalaya, one of the most prominent institutions for Vedic education in the country.

'In fact, it was at Karamveer's insistence that we designed a postgraduate course in yoga in the first place,' said Professor Ishwar Bharadwaj, who has been the head of department of human consciousness and yogic sciences at the university since the 1980s. Bharadwaj remembers Karamveer as a diligent student who aspired to take yoga to the masses. 'Karamveer had a much wider canvas in mind for yoga at the time.' It was Karamveer's vision for yoga that enlivened Ramdev and laid the foundations of his empire.

Gurukul Kangri Vishwavidyalaya's postgraduate course in yoga, the first in the country, was started in 1991 – it was around this time that Karamveer met Balkrishna. That year just three students took up the course. One of Karamveer's two classmates, Surakshit Goswami, later became an acclaimed yoga teacher and writer at the *Times of India*. 'I don't see him often any more, but I remember Karamveer was a gentle, well-respected man. He has remained a moral man,' says Goswami.

~

The improbable friendship grew as the months passed. When Balkrishna faced financial difficulties, he asked Karamveer for help – a letter of introduction to some members of the Arya Samaj Society in Porbunder. Armed with this introduction from his well-regarded friend, Balkrishna treated several patients in Porbunder with Ayurvedic medicines and quickly became famous there.

'It just happened,' Acharya Balkrishna says with a smile. His prognoses for some patients turned out to be accurate, and 'Suddenly, hordes of people, Hindus and Muslims, were coming to me in my clinic there [in Porbunder]. In Nepal, while growing up, I had not always want to become an Ayurveda doctor, you know.'

The successful stint in Porbunder buoyed Balkrishna, made him hopeful of things to come. Still, even as late as in 1993, Balkrishna did not know what he really wanted to do with his life. 'I'd never dreamed of becoming a vaidya or anything. It just happened,' he says.

Around that time, towards the end of 1993 or in early 1994, something happened in the faraway gurukul Kishangarh in Haryana that would bring their third to-be partner to Haridwar.

After graduating from gurukul Kalwa, Acharya Ramdev – he had adopted the name Ramdev when he joined the Khanpur gurukul – took up the post of teacher at another Arya Samaj gurukul, Kishangarh Ghasera. The hardened son of a hard man, Ramdev now wielded power in an institution that allowed him to beat his students when they disobeyed him in any way.

'Like everyone else, even I had heard of his famed propensity for rage and violence,' said the author of Ramdev's 'official' biography, Sandeep Dev. 'He may not share it now,' says Dev, but Ramdev had told him of an incident that illustrated his furious temper and led to his exit from Kishangarh. It has been recounted in Dev's book:

> At his gurukul, one of his students had stolen something. Seething with rage, Ramdev picked up a sheesham stick and began beating the boy so hard and for so long that the boy was left in a critical condition. The boy's body was in shreds, blood flowing freely from his wounds. Seeing the boy's condition, Ramdev felt a sudden compassion. He said he was very upset and angry with himself, remorse gripped him. So, he left.

Others say Ramdev fled from a fight in Kishangarh. An uncomfortable silence descends on Kishangarh residents when asked about the incident. They are unwilling to discuss Ramdev as he has taken over the gurukul and is now their employer.

Whatever his reasons for departing from Kishangarh, Ramdev soon arrived in Haridwar, where his junior from gurukul Kalwa, Acharya Balkrishna, had found a mentor, Karamveer, and a place to live in.

Ramdev managed to secure a place in Karamveer's coterie through the recommendation of Balkrishna. 'He [Balkrishna] came to me and said there was another person he knew, who sang very well. I thought it will be good to have a singer in our midst... so I said, "Well, go get him then,'" recalls Karamveer. 'When he [Ramdev] came, I told him that if he wanted to stay with me, he would have to take two oaths: lifelong celibacy and free service of the people. He would not accept money in exchange for his service or teaching. Those were my conditions ... Ramdev took the pledge.'

Ramdev's arrival in Haridwar brought the cast of characters together. Acharya Karamveer took Ramdev and Balkrishna totally under his wing, and taught them many things, including how to teach yoga, especially to large groups of people. Karamveer's instruction and the legitimacy that Ramdev and Balkrishna derived from their closeness to him, a respected academic, were invaluable for them, especially as they themselves did not have recognized degrees.

Though it was to be a short-lived partnership, the curtain was about to rise on a riveting performance that would grab national attention.

4

The Guru

Kankhal, Haridwar, 1990–95

Situated along the old Ganga canal, the Kripalu Bagh Ashram complex had become a fruit orchard where litchis and mangoes grew. The once-bustling ashram that had sheltered revolutionaries fighting the British Raj had fallen silent.

While a gurukul is an institution of education, an ashram is a monastery, spiritual retreat or hermitage. An ashram can sometimes operate a gurukul under its umbrella, but their primary purposes are distinct. Each ashram can have its own rules, regulations and its own set of spiritual beliefs and traditions.

Bereft of young blood, Kripalu Bagh Ashram's descent into irrelevance was slow and steady. A lifelong Kankhal resident reminisces, 'I'd been seeing Shankar

Dev at that Kripalu Bagh Ashram for over forty-five years. As children, we spent afternoons swimming downstream in our shorts and raiding orchards on both sides of the stream. An old ascetic used to live there, but we hardly ever saw him. It was always his disciple and the ashram caretaker, Shankar Dev, who chased us away, wildly waving a stick at us.'

When that old sadhu died, Shankar Dev had to shoulder the responsibility of running the ashram. Born in Almora in 1929, Shankar Dev took deeksha (initiation into a religious order) from his guru sometime in 1958 and began to wear saffron robes. He came to Haridwar in 1968 and stayed there for the rest of his life.

'Shankar Dev was illiterate and not a worldly man,' says Sushant Mahendru, another lifelong resident of Kankhal whose grandfather Om Prakash Jigyasu was an old friend of Shankar Dev's. Shankar Dev played an important role in helping install the three new friends into Kripalu Bagh Ashram. 'Maharaj Shankar Devji came to our house for breakfast every day for twenty years until my grandfather passed away in 2002. With him, Ramdev, Karamveer and Balkrishna also came. After my grandfather's death, Shankar Dev came less often, but he still came. We saw it all happen to him, up close,' Mahendru trails off.

Shankar Dev was a man of simple needs, but he had to make ends meet. So he took on tenants at the ashram.

Thirteen to fourteen tenants lived in hodgepodge rooms, built one on top of the other in the ashram complex and 'the rent they paid was enough for Shankar Dev. He didn't need more. He didn't even want more,' says Mahendru. 'He hardly had any expenses, so the money had just kept accumulating over the years. He travelled around on his cycle. By 1994, he'd told my grandfather that he had accumulated a tidy four to five lakh rupees in his account to look after him in his old age.'

Nearly seventy years old, Shankar Dev was brooding on the fate of his ashram. 'He was worried about the tenants,' remembers Mahendru. 'He believed they would usurp the property after he was gone. He did not want that to happen. He was looking for someone deserving to give it to. At this late stage, he was looking for a disciple.'

Shankar Dev used to sit on a cot and watch the world go by. He was especially aware of, and had observed, one young man who frequently rode by on a cycle, on his way to university: Karamveer. Shankar Dev had made up his mind. He would leave the ashram to Karamveer.

'Maharajji [Shankar Dev] was very kind to me,' remembers Karamveer. 'He used to tell me how worried he was that the tenants would usurp the ashram. He wanted me to become his disciple and take it over.'

But Karamveer politely declined: 'Maharajji, you worship idols and ring bells and all that. I could never do it. I am an Arya Samaji. We won't be able to get along.' Shankar Dev was not dissuaded. Maybe Karamveer's refusal to accept the ashram, when others would have grabbed the opportunity, only made him surer of his decision.

Shankar Dev noticed the young man's newly acquired friends. They were a hard-working trio: renting utensils to make chawanprash at the Tripura Yog Ashram of Swami Amlanand in Kankhal where they lived, hawking it on cycles, collecting herbs from nearby forests.

'We were trying to see if we could build something together,' recalls Karamveer. Over those eighteen to twenty months between 1993 and 1995, they travelled once to Gangotri and conducted at least two medical camps in the tribal regions of Assam, where they offered medicines for diseases typical to the region.

'It was in the winter of 1994, during our second camp in Assam, that Ramdev said to me that if we wanted to offer free services ... to people, we should have a base of our own. He asked, "Why don't you accept Shankar Dev's offer? We will be able to do more if we have a base to operate out of." His question made me think. It was a practical idea and it did make sense,' recalls Karamveer.

So, from the jungles of Assam, they wrote a letter to Shankar Dev telling him that they were willing to take over the ashram, that they would take on the tenants and drive them out, and revive Kripalu Bagh with action and industry.

Shankar Dev was delighted that Karamveer was willing. "'I don't know your friends, but I know you. I'm trusting you,' he had told me,' says Karamveer, staring fixedly at some long-ago moment.

On 5 January 1995 Ramdev, Balkrishna and Karamveer registered the Divya Yog Mandir Trust in Kankhal, Haridwar. Swami Shankar Dev was listed in the trust deed as its *Sanrakshak* (convener), Acharya Ramdev as its *Adhyaksh* (president), Acharya Karamveer as its *Upadhyaksh* (vice-president) and Acharya Balkrishna as the *Mahamantri* (general secretary).

Immediately, a legal battle was commenced to drive out the tenants. Shankar Dev's old friend Om Prakash Jigyasu, who was also a board member listed on the trust deed, put them in touch with his lawyer, Vijay Kumar Sharma, to help them. Mahendru recalls that an out-of-court settlement was arrived at with the tenants.

Divya Yog Mandir was ready to start out on its listed mission: 'Teaching yoga to the masses in practical way, in order to help people achieve the good health, sound minds and great bliss.' Well, almost ready.

Kankhal, Baisakhi day, 9 April 1995

One order of business was still pending. In keeping with tradition, someone had to accept discipleship from Shankar Dev to become heir to the ashram.

According to the Hindu ashram tradition, only a disciple can lead the ashram after the guru dies. This ensures that the ashram's traditions and founding precepts don't fade away. Karamveer had already refused to become Shankar Dev's disciple because he was an Arya Samaj follower.

Ramdev was also from the Arya Samaj school of thought and, on the face of it, had the same ideological differences with Shankar Dev. But ever-pragmatic, Ramdev understood that refusal to accept discipleship could mean losing the ashram. If there were ideological differences, Ramdev was willing to lay them aside and compromise in order to consolidate their tenuous new hold on stability.

So he agreed to accept the saffron robes from Shankar Dev and become his shishya. Despite Ramdev's hardheadedness and cool pragmatism, this decision must have been sobering. Still in his twenties, Ramdev was agreeing to a life of sanyas, complete renunciation.

Although various Hindu religious texts have different interpretations of what life after renunciation entails, there are some basics they all agree on. Ramdev knew he was closing some doors forever: he would have to be celibate for the rest of his life, was forbidden to marry, would have to withdraw from his family, shun material wealth, willingly embrace poverty, and never seek fame.

But being a renunciate came with its own benefits: Ramdev's new saffron robes would automatically confer upon him great respectability and ensure that people would judge him by a different yardstick. After all, he was giving up everything personal to serve humankind.

On 9 April 1995, Acharya Ramdev's family, friends, teachers, colleagues and students gathered on the banks of the river Ganga in Kankhal to witness the ceremony in which he would cast off the white clothes of the brahmachari – which denote celibacy before marriage, but also hold the promise of family life in the future – and adopt the saffron robes of the sanyasi.

Professor Ishwar Bharadwaj, Karamveer's teacher at university, remembers warning his student at that time, 'You may be Ramdev's mentor. But now you are wearing white clothes. He is wearing bhagwa [saffron]. People will touch his feet – not yours.'

Karamveer recollects scoffing at the cautionary words. 'I planned to do so [take sanyas] at some point, but back then, I did not feel I was ready to take that step. It would have been dishonest and hypocritical if I had taken such a big step for the sake of appearances alone,' says Karamveer, who eventually did take sanyas.

But Ishwar Bharadwaj's comment was prescient of things to come.

5

The Early Days

Kripalu Bagh Ashram, 1996–97

Work began in earnest. Old residents of Haridwar remember them well – cycling around town, making and selling chawanprash, going to people's homes to perform havans. 'Ramdevji had a good voice,' recalls Dr Veena Shastri, principal of the Mahila Mahavidyalaya women's college in Kankhal. They were also busy organizing the first of their yoga camps.

At first Ramdev and Karamveer toured Gujarat: Karamveer taught yoga and Ramdev sang bhajans – all the while observing, learning the art of teaching yoga. He was a quick learner. When they returned to the ashram, they began to hold local yoga camps as well.

Sharad Kumar Gupta, owner of a Bharat Gas agency in Haridwar, remembers attending the first local camp, sometime in 1997. 'About ten–twelve people had gathered at Kripalu Bagh Ashram in Kankhal, where Ramdev was setting up his class under litchi trees,' says Gupta.

At that camp, Ramdev did the teaching, while Karamveer stepped back and watched his student evolve as an instructor. Many remember Karamveer taking notes while Ramdev taught yoga – keeping track of the errors he made while teaching the class.

The ashram seemed to run on a shoestring budget back then: another resident recalls that while Ramdev sat on some pieces of plastic, his students did yoga on the bare ground.

When the week-long camp ended, Gupta says he donated a blue tarpaulin for the next batch of students to sit on. The second camp began the day after the first ended. This time thirty people attended. Gupta also gave Ramdev a microphone and speakers to make teaching a larger gathering possible. At their third camp, 150 people showed up. Soon there was not enough space to accommodate everyone who wanted to attend their camps.

As Ramdev and Karamveer steadily built their reputation for yoga, Balkrishna was busy too. Although he held no medical degrees, his interest in Ayurveda drew him to its practice. He remembered the success

The Early Days

he'd had in Porbunder and was trying to establish a clinic within the ashram.

But there was a problem. Since he had no formal degree or training, under the provisions of the Drugs and Cosmetics Act, 1945, he could not get a licence to run either an Ayurvedic clinic or a manufacturing unit. The problem did not stump him for long. By December 1995 itself, they had found a silent partner and convinced him to let them use his licence as cover for Divya Yog Mandir Trust's Divya Pharmacy. As long as the licence holder remained a 'technical supervisor', the manufacturing unit would be legally clear.

In a small single-storey house up the canal from their ashram, on the other side of the bridge, there lived an ageing vaidya, a sanyasi called Swami Yogananda. Formerly N.P. Singh, he was trained as an Ayurvedic bhisag, or physician. This qualified him to practice as a vaidya and manufacture Ayurvedic drugs.

According to Karamveer, 'Swami Yogananda was a friend of mine from Aligarh and he agreed to allow us to register Divya Pharmacy using his licence. It was important to keep one vaidya on the registration.' This was the only way the government would allow them to register the pharmacy.

Armed with Yogananda's licence and Karamveer's mentorship, Balkrishna set up a tiny tin-shed manufacturing unit of Divya Pharmacy in the ashram. In a long room, qualified Ayurvedic doctors whom the pharmacy had hired would diagnose patients. Advertised as a free clinic, the medical consultation was indeed free – but the medicines were not.

'In 2002, when I joined them, the doctors were instructed to write up medicines for no less than 1500 rupees,' said Vipin Pradhan, Karamveer's nephew and a former aide who left the team in 2005. 'What they were told to charge in the years before that, I do not know.' While Rs 1500 may seem like an awful lot to be charged for medicine at an Ayurvedic clinic in 2002 in Haridwar, Pradhan insists that he has got the figure right.

This economic model remains unchanged even today: at any of the 5000 Patanjali chikitsalayas, or clinics, that dot the country, the consultations are free but medicines are charged for.

At first, they did not have much manufacturing capacity. It is an open secret in Haridwar that Divya Pharmacy medicines were sourced from some other local pharmacists. Karamveer confirmed that Divya Pharmacy did not produce all their medicines themselves and bought some from other Ayurvedic pharmacies, such as Adarsh Pharmacy, and sold these forward.

But Divya Pharmacy still managed to build up quite a reputation. People from around Haridwar, from as far as Dehradun, heard of the unusual, free Ayurvedic clinic where the doctors did not charge consulting fees, and made their way to Kripalu Bagh Ashram. Most Ayurvedic doctors, including the promoter of Adarsh Pharmacy, had more conventional practices, where you paid for the consultation as well as the medicine.

Shankar Dev looked on with quiet satisfaction as his derelict ashram began to resonate with the hum of new industry.

~

Dehradun, 1998

Radhika Nagrath was a bright, young computer programmer at Aptech in Dehradun when she first brought her mother to Kripalu Bagh Ashram for a check-up in 1998. When Balkrishna discovered that she was a computer engineer, he begged her to make their website for them. Six months later, she agreed to help.

Nagrath remembers simpler days. She 'helped them design their logo ... told them what a logo was, why they should have one ... They were lovely days, before it got so big. We'd go to the jungles around Haridwar, talk about medicines, they were very carefree days,' she reminisces.

Still, money was tight and Balkrishna kept close tabs on the expenses. 'I remember once Swamiji [Baba

Ramdev] took a paper with a letterhead to scribble something ... Acharya Balkrishnaji yelled at him and said, "Yeh kharab kar diya ... do rupaiya ka paper! [You have ruined this – Rs 2 worth of paper!]"'

Over the next decade, the soft-spoken Radhika Nagrath became more and more intertwined with their enterprise and watched it grow. Even though she continues to work with Divya Pharmacy, while also freelancing for major English-language national dailies, she remains an outsider and a cool observer of Balkrishna and Ramdev's phenomenal rise, though with obvious affection for them.

'Soon after Baba Ramdev set up, his family moved here. His mother and brother came to live in Kankhal. From the very beginning, his brother Ram Bharat was in charge of the money,' Nagrath remembers.

Ramdev's sister also soon came to live with them. 'Groundwater levels were depleting fast in our village,' remembers Devdutt Yadav, Ramdev's older brother. 'Living off the land was becoming harder. Every year, the well had to be dug deeper to find the receding groundwater under the earth ... so the family had to find another way – go to Haridwar.'

The brothers put their young sister in a women's college, in the care of Dr Veena Shastri. 'Ramdevji requested me to take care of her. Since there were many young men at the ashram, he felt it was not an

The Early Days

appropriate place for his sister. I remember her brother Ram Bharat used to bring milk for her from the ashram in the morning. He used to come on a cycle to the hostel gate to deliver it,' says Dr Shastri.

Locals watched as the new owners of Kripalu Bagh Ashram grew into money during those years – their cycle swiftly replaced by a brown Bajaj Chetak scooter, then a white Gypsy, a cherry-coloured Maruti and so on.

Ramdev and Karamveer were still building their reputations as yoga teachers and most of their camps were free or charged nominal fees. The money at this stage was said to be coming from Divya Pharmacy. 'I've deposited sacksful of cash, donations and loans, I think, for them during those years,' recalls Mahendru, who was seventeen at the time. 'Handing them to me, Ramdev used to say, "Beta, go drop these off at the bank while I talk to your grandfather."'

It did not escape young Sushant Mahendru's notice that their guru Shankar Dev, former owner of Kripalu Bagh Ashram, still travelled on his bicycle.

6

Aastha Television

Mumbai, April 2000

Far from Haridwar and the fledgling Divya Yog Mandir Trust and its pharmacy, a meeting was taking place that would transform Ramdev's life.

Madhav Kant Mishra, an Allahabad journalist from a devout family, had an idea. In a television landscape dominated by soap operas – unending dramas of beautifully dressed mothers-in-law and daughters-in-law – he saw an opportunity for something quite different. 'From a very young age I was drawn to spirituality and I felt this void needed to be filled. I was carrying around the idea of Aastha in my mind for a very long time,' he says.

He took the idea to Kirit Mehta, chairman and managing director of CMM Broadcasting Network

Limited, a production studio with mounting debts and 11,000 square feet of space. But Mehta had other plans. He was about to launch the music channel CMM Music – those were the heyday of MTV, Channel V and VH1 – and laughed at Mishra's idea. And he wasn't the only one. 'Everyone, all my friends, were asking me, "What are you doing? Who is going to watch some dharam-karam channel?" At that time I told him [Mehta]: "In six months' time, your music channel will shut down and this channel will run your show."'

Mehta, a second-generation businessman – whose assets were under dispute at that time, with several lenders, including IDBI Bank, demanding repayment of loans – slowly came to see the potential in Mishra's vision. He decided to invest in this new venture called Aastha Broadcasting Network Limited. But instead of investing in Aastha directly, he routed his investment through companies owned by his wife, son and daughter, adding up to 50 per cent of Aastha. The other half of the capital came in April 2000 from Santosh Kumar Jain, a Kolkata-based chartered accountant and investor.

Mehta and Jain each handed over one per cent of their shares to the broker Hiren Harshad Doshi, who helped hammer the deal through which the company was formed.

On 18 June 2000, the day Aastha went live for the first time, the three promoters performed a havan in

Aastha Television

Delhi. A new chapter of Indian television was about to unfold.

'I knew there was a market. But even I did not anticipate how successful it would become,' says Mishra, who was appointed Aastha's North India editor-in-chief based in Delhi, handling content, creating shows and also scouring the northern countryside for new faces to feature on the channel. Six months later, Aastha made history when it telecast the Maha Kumbh Mela live from Mishra's hometown of Allahabad. When ratings shot up, a realization sank in: they may have something big on their hands, after all.

Within a month of Aastha's launch came Sanskar, another religious channel. 'It was only a difference of days,' says Dilip Kabra, a key promoter of Sanskar. Clearly, religious broadcasting was an idea whose time had come and by 2006 there were no fewer than ten such channels in India. Madhav Kant Mishra's prediction had come true.

~

Soon after Aastha Broadcasting Network Limited was set up, Kirit Mehta set up Aastha International which in turn owned Aastha UK and Aastha USA. Aastha International was a totally separate company from Aastha Broadcasting Network Ltd, or Aastha India for short. The former was wholly owned, run and set up by Mehta. It exclusively beamed Aastha India's content in the US and UK.

But trouble was brewing for the promoters of Aastha India, especially Kirit Mehta: a sudden jump in the price of Aastha shares – from Rs 9.70 in November 2000 to Rs 39.10 in February 2001 – raised the suspicions of the Securities and Exchange Board of India (SEBI). Upon investigation, it was found that the promoters had indulged in illegalities and grossly violated SEBI regulations. As a result, in an interim order passed in September 2005, SEBI froze the sale or purchase of 93 per cent of Aastha's shares till January 2007.

7

The TV Star

Haridwar, 2000–02

At the turn of the millennium, yoga had a moment of runaway success. Suddenly, it was cool again to be a yogi. After the heady love affair that the west had with India and its godmen in the 1970s, things had cooled off considerably. This was, if you will, a second fling.

Celebrities in the west embraced its practice and yoga captured the world's imagination. In an interview on Oprah Winfrey's talk show in 1998, Madonna said discovering Ashtanga Yoga while she was pregnant had 'centred' her. Oprah, then one of America's most significant and powerful taste makers, also brought renowned yogi Rodney Yee on her show in 2001. She was so taken by its practice that she started a company-sponsored weekly yoga class for her employees. An April

2001 *Time* magazine story, 'The Power of Yoga', featuring supermodel Christy Turlington on the cover, estimated that about 15 million Americans were practising yoga. Naturally, the growing American obsession renewed Indian interest in yoga.

And while well-heeled Indians acquired yoga instructors, the rest of India had neither access to good yoga teachers nor the money to pay for them. The travelling yoga teachers Ramdev and Karamveer did not miss the surging crowds clamouring to attend their yoga camps.

Seeing the increasing curiosity about yoga, especially among the elites, in 2000 Ramdev and Karamveer organized a free yoga camp for local authorities in Haridwar. The Haridwar superintendent of police and the district magistrate attended this very successful week-long session at Bhalla College. From this point on, befriending government officials and politicians, both in and out of power, would become a trademark growth strategy of Baba Ramdev's.

All the ingredients were in place: a global momentum was building behind yoga, religious television channels were on the rise and there was a huge dearth of good yoga teachers. The stage was set for the right yoga guru to take his place on the stage.

Madhav Kant Mishra was paying attention. 'I knew that just having swamis talking and lecturing on television was not going to be enough ... Anything to do with yoga and health would do well,' he remembers.

So he went looking for the right yoga guru for Aastha. 'I had three choices,' he recalls. Karamveer, Ramdev and a third local yoga teacher based near Haridwar. 'But only one of them was a saffron-robed guru,' he says, smiling. 'The optics of that were promising because I knew our audience would prefer to learn from a sanyasi.' Karamveer, Ramdev's mentor, had lost out to his protégé.

Mishra's hunt for an orange-robed yoga teacher brought him to Kripalu Bagh Ashram. 'When I saw Ramdev do that nauli kriya, churning his stomach ... I knew he would be a big hit,' says Mishra. He made a recording of Ramdev teaching yoga and sent it to Aastha's promoters in Mumbai for the green light to put Ramdev on air.

~

Mumbai, 2002

Unimpressed with what they saw of Ramdev on that tape, Aastha promoter Kirit Mehta and CEO Ajit Gupta refused to air it. They simply said, 'What boss? He moves his stomach around like that ... it won't work.'

It is not clear how Ramdev handled their rejection, but the idea of teaching yoga on television had fired his imagination. Within a few short weeks of discovering how the television business worked for swamis like him, he went to the rival Sanskar channel and secured himself twenty minutes of airtime at 6.45 a.m. by paying for it.

Religious television channels had an unusual business model at that time. Unlike normal television networks that have to rely on advertisers, religious channels had access to a never-before-tapped revenue stream: the godmen themselves. Flush with funds from donations, these gurus saw in Aastha an opportunity not only to rally their bases, but also to recruit new converts.

According to Mishra, within a year of its launch, the idealism that had spurred Aastha had faded. Religious gurus had quickly understood that TV was the most powerful way to reach people – inside their homes. 'A situation evolved where religious gurus believed that if they wanted to survive in the religious marketplace, they had to be on Aastha. I will not take names, but religious gurus used to come to us and discuss their rivals – "Oh, you are running this guy? How much is he paying you? I will pay more."' Aastha's and Sanskar's airtime was being auctioned, offered to the highest bidder.

'The real gurus never made it on the channel. Even if they made a brief appearance, they didn't survive. They could not pay, you see,' says a matter-of-fact Mishra.

'The channel simply became a medium for campaigning for new devotees. The promoters of all those channels thought there is no better business than this. It is unfortunate that they made no effort to exploit the aspects of their trade that were viable. No effort was made to get advertisers and focus on content.' His voice is still sad at the lost promise and opportunity. Back then, there were few takers for Mishra's principled reflections. Money was pouring in. And no one was complaining about where it was coming from.

This business model made it simple for Ramdev to shop for airtime with Sanskar channel, where a twenty-minute slot cost Rs 1,50,000. Kabra, a key promoter of Sanskar, remembers his first meeting with Ramdev in Delhi with his manager, Gopal Maheshwari. Ramdev told them he could not pay the entire amount right away but he assured them that he would generate enough viewership to be able to pay them back.

Where Mehta had refused to venture, Kabra decided to plunge in and take a chance on Ramdev. 'There was something compelling about Ramdevji from the very beginning,' he says.

The first of Ramdev's yoga shivirs, or camps, to be telecast on Sanskar was conducted in Haridwar. Knowing how much was riding on it, Ramdev must have been nervous, but his performance was sensational and his chemistry with the audience undeniable. He was the saffron-clad Pied Piper who could make his stomach churn and ripple, wrap his legs around his neck and dazzle viewers with dreams of eternal youth and instant good health. His audience was enchanted, and followed him into a dream land where cancer, homosexuality and HIV could be 'cured' by yoga, grey hair turned black, and the divine experienced. During that first shivir itself, he appealed to people for donations and was not disappointed. Two people in the live audience gave him cheques for Rs 5 lakh each, several times the amount he owed Sanskar for that time slot.

When Ramdev's slot helped drive up Sanskar's TRP ratings, the folks at Aastha wondered: Had they made a mistake by passing him up? By July 2003 Television Audience Measurement Media Research reported that Sanskar had 6.9 million viewers. Aastha trailed behind at second position with 5.7 million viewers. Ramdev's trademark nauli kriya, an entrancing rippling of the stomach, had clearly worked. The viewers were hooked.

Realizing their mistake in letting Ramdev go, Mishra swung into action to convince Ramdev to abandon Sanskar and come to Aastha instead. Sometime towards the end of 2003 Ramdev left Sanskar due to personal differences with one of its promoters and started appearing on air exclusively on Aastha. Realizing it was a huge blunder to let Ramdev go, Kabra told Sanskar's board they were making a mistake. 'I knew Swamiji's

The TV Star

star was rising and he was only at the beginning of it. He was about to take off like a rocket.' But despite his best efforts, Kabra could do nothing to stop Ramdev's departure. As he had predicted, millions of viewers migrated with Ramdev to Aastha. Sanskar's owners in turn decided they would never feature Ramdev on their channel again.

Over the next few years, mornings in India changed. Millions of families which could not afford to hire a personal yoga trainer and did not even possibly know where to find one woke up early to greet Baba Ramdev – the swami who came to teach them at home on the television.

Ramdev stripped ancient teachings of their obscure trappings and made them accessible again. Unlike other swamis, he did not mystify yoga and pranayama as sacred, rites that unlocked the doors of spiritual realms. His was a simpler creed that said: here is an easy code using which you can live in a healthy body. If you have a healthy body, you can do whatever you like with it. He steered clear of religious controversy or recommendations.

The ancient texts on yoga and pranayama are powerful tools left to us hundreds of years ago. The breathing techniques prescribed in pranayama have made their way into the global arsenal to battle diseases such as diabetes and heart problems. Health coach Matt

Traverso in his book *Reverse Diabetes Now!* says 'optimal breathing' or 'deep diaphragmatic breathing' reinstates the oxygen supply in the blood and ensures lymph stimulation. Both these are wonderful tools in allowing your body to fight chronic diseases, clinical studies show. The technique for 'deep diaphragmatic breathing' is one of the pranic kriyas prescribed by the ancient sage Patanjali, who wrote the Patanjali Yog Sutras 1600 years ago. His Ashtanga Yoga, or the eightfold path of yoga, is the foundation of Baba Ramdev's teachings.

Working primarily with the first four steps of Patanjali's eightfold path – yama, niyama, asana and pranayama – Ramdev taught people that they could master their own health. Coming from a world of poverty himself, he understood that making ends meet was a full-time job. He knew that it left no time to meditate and ponder the imponderables of existence and contemplate the truths of life. So he kept it simple and down to earth. He taught Indians that being healthy does not have to be expensive or time-consuming. He reminded them that their own heritage offered solutions – ranging from anulom-vilom (deep diaphragmatic breathing) and kapalbhati pranayama (releasing toxins from the body through forceful breathing) to a series of asanas for a variety of ailments – that could easily be adopted in a modern world to live a healthy, peaceful life.

The TV Star

How could such a formula, this confluence of ancient and modern, not work? It truly was an idea whose time had come. Millions of people benefited from Ramdev's teachings on the television. Millions learned how to manage their ailments.

And those whose lives he changed became incredibly grateful and devoted to him. Ramdev's success is of course a testament to yoga and the power of mass media, but it is also a credit to him. He was unique in that he sold people a dream of good health. And Ramdev's path to it was practical, simple and cost-effective.

It is hard not to speculate what he must have felt about his heady success. Where others might have lost their head with all the attention and frittered away opportunity, Ramdev clearly didn't. He saw the power of television and worked his way towards becoming a media house owner. Today Ramdev owns both Sanskar and Aastha, the mediums that made his success possible. 'There is no greater illustration of the great business of religion than this,' says Mishra.

8

Friends in High Places

Dehradun, Uttarakhand, 2003–04

While Ramdev was busy with his television appearances, Balkrishna was hard at work consolidating and tweaking their Ayurveda enterprise.

The licence of Divya Pharmacy had come up for its yearly renewal in 2003. After eight years of operating under the licence of N.P. Singh (known then as Swami Yogananda), the alliance was abruptly dropped in 2003. The Divya Pharmacy licence was renewed using the credentials of other vaidyas who were now their employees. Vaidya Yogananda was said to be unhappy and feeling neglected and bypassed by Ramdev and company, but amid the first flush of success, no one had time for disgruntled old allies.

The Divya Pharmacy website claimed to possess

cures for 140 diseases – including HIV, cancer, diabetes, epilepsy and impotency. Under Balkrishna's watch, the Kankhal pharmacy was running like a well-oiled business machine. Two dozen hired vaidyas inspected patients swiftly – for free – and prescribed medicines that had to be purchased from Divya Pharmacy. The pharmacy always made sure that its patients signed legal disclaimers, releasing the ashram from consequences in case of adverse reactions.

Ramdev's soaring popularity meant that more and more people from all round the country came to attend his yoga shivirs. In the encampments would be doctors from Balkrishna's team who travelled with Ramdev, ready to diagnose ailments and treat as many people as possible after the yoga sessions. Then there were those patients who went straight to the source, the Kankhal ashram, and waited in long queues outside its walls, looking for natural cures to varied illnesses. Beyond the gates of Kripalu Bagh Ashram waited Balkrishna and his team of physicians, ready to translate Ramdev's growing fame into profit.

Politicians and businessmen were quick to sense the new power rising in Haridwar. They came bearing gifts, offers of friendship, proposals for alliances. Ramdev shrewdly recognized the two people who could do the most for him – the colourful chief minister of Uttarakhand, Narayan Dutt Tiwari, and fellow Yadav and chief minister of Uttar Pradesh, Mulayam Singh – both of whom took him under their wing.

Ramdev also started making canny and strategic donations on behalf of the Divya Yog Mandir Trust to politically connected NGOs, perhaps to gain favour with influential men in the establishment. The *Indian Express* reported that one of his tax-free donations, of Rs 25 lakh, was made to Himjyoti, an NGO founded and run by a foundation set up by the then Uttarakhand governor, Sudershan Agarwal.

'Business boomed,' recollects Vipin Pradhan, who, as mentioned earlier, lived and worked in the ashram between 2002 and 2005. The number of doctors on Divya Pharmacy's rolls increased, but medicines bought from other pharmacists were simply not enough.

Pradhan recalls, 'We were all, all of us young men who worked there, watching a trickle of money swell into a stream that year. We sat around every night for hours counting money. I remember counting Rs 22 lakh in one single night. By May 2004, we refused to count any more. So they brought in a note-counting machine.'

But that financial year, 2004–05, Divya Pharmacy filed yearly sales of only Rs 6,73,000 and paid sales tax of Rs 53,000. When a suspicious sales tax office investigated, they found enough evidence (2000 kilos of papers) to initiate a raid. 'There was a clear-cut case of evasion. Trading, sales, so much of his business activities were just not recorded on his books,' said the then sales tax deputy commissioner Jitender Rana, who headed the investigation.

According to Rana, Divya Pharmacy had evaded sales tax to the tune of Rs 5 crore. This would put their estimated sales somewhere in the ballpark of Rs 60 crore.

But after the raid Governor Sudershan Agarwal allegedly got involved on behalf of Ramdev. Rana says he came under tremendous pressure: 'The governor began breathing down my neck, asking me to meet him. Such a request was highly improper because as an officer heading an investigation, I could not go to him to discuss an ongoing case. I informed the chief minister about the governor wanting to meet me. The governor then demanded an enquiry into the raid.'

Such vehement opposition from a high-ranking constitutional official apparently knocked the morale of the investigating officers. Eventually, says Rana, 'I was forced to leave. I took VRS [voluntary retirement scheme] even though I had four years of service still left because it became very difficult to live. Too many people in power were protecting Ramdev ... I came to my senses and left.'

'There was no dearth of people who wanted to give land and resources to Babaji,' remembers Pradhan. 'He had well-connected patrons among the business houses as well. The Poddars, Hindujas and Subrata Roy.'

As Ramdev was transforming from a simple travelling yoga teacher to a celebrity of sorts, it became clear to everyone he was not someone to be messed with. Kripalu Bagh Ashram was also no longer large enough to accommodate their growing business and ambitions. So when the sick and bankrupt Yogi Pharmacy's building by the railway tracks in Haridwar went up for sale that year, Ramdev and Balkrishna emerged as its new owners after the gavel fell.

9

Mystery 1: The Ally's Murder

Kankhal, 27 December 2004

A day after the Asian tsunami swept up the shorelines of fourteen countries, killing nearly a quarter of a million people, an intriguing event occurred in Kankhal. In the darkening winter evening of 27 December 2004, a scuffle broke out in the single-storey Yogananda Ashram, home to Swami Yogananda, the man whose licence had enabled Divya Pharmacy to function and grow for eight years since its inception in 1995 till 2003.

Yogananda's neighbours are cagey about discussing it even today but they say they heard raised voices coming from his house that eventful evening. No one imagined, though, that Yogananda – the lonely man who lived without a telephone or even electricity – was being knifed to death. One Vasant Kumar Singh discovered his lifeless body shortly after and called the police. Along with other neighbours, the young Tarun Kumar went in with the police. 'I remember it still. He was there, in that dark room when I went in . . . lying in a pool of his own blood.'

As mentioned earlier, in 2003 Divya Pharmacy had abruptly changed the vaidya on its registration from Swami Yogananda to Sri Saty Pal Singh. Yogananda is said to have had a falling out with Ramdev's increasingly powerful enterprise but the reasons for this are still unknown.

With Yogananda's death, a key associate who had provided critical help to Ramdev in his early days was gone. The murder remains unsolved till date. Ten months later, on 25 October 2005, investigating officer B.B. Juyal filed his final report in the case – Case unsolved. Perpetrators unknown.

10

A New Mentor Enters

Bhopal and Nashik, 2004

Within a year or two of his debut on television, Ramdev instinctively knew his audience. He also knew that his content had to remain fresh if he hoped to keep his growing following. His hunt for new content and the necessity to keep his TV appearances novel and interesting led him to Rajeev Dixit.

Few in cosmopolitan living rooms of India would have heard of this charismatic young man. But Dixit, a well-read and compelling orator with a round face and large, kind eyes, drew thousands of followers from all around the country into a Gandhian organization called Azadi Bachao Andolan. Its website declares it is 'a national movement in India to counter the onslaught of foreign multinationals and the western culture on

Indians, their values, and on the Indian economy in general'. Sounds remarkably similar to what Ramdev says today.

Dixit is considered the architect of a modern swadeshi movement in India and Ramdev openly accepts that his own swadeshi rhetoric and narrative are drawn from Rajeev Dixit's research. Ramdev's current attack on multinationals is just an echo of Dixit's words.

Born in Nah village in Uttar Pradesh, Dixit was pursuing a BTech degree in Allahabad when the Bhopal gas tragedy occurred. He began thinking and asking questions about what had brought Union Carbide to India in the first place and about the economic compulsions that forced Indians to allow multinationals to set up their plants in the country. These questions led him to Dharampal, a Gandhian thinker, who shaped his economic worldview.

Seven years later, in January 1992, Dixit founded the Azadi Bachao Andolan in Wardha. The khadi-clad Dixit took to touring the country, giving thousands of lectures and speeches in elegant Hindi. Over the next several years, he stitched together and refined his argument against multinational companies and claimed that liberalization and globalization were the modern faces of colonialism. His organization recorded his speeches, and sold cassettes and later CDs of them wherever they could.

A New Mentor Enters

With 10 crore supporters and a presence in 1500 tehsils across the country, the Azadi Bachao Andolan became an object of envy for anyone looking to build an army of followers.

Cleary, Dixit would be a valuable ally for Ramdev to have.

Sometime in February 2004, according to K.N. Govindacharya, then a Rashtriya Swayamsevak Sangh (RSS) ideologue, 'I ran into Ramdev somewhere in Bhopal and he told me he was looking for Rajeev Dixit. So I made a call.' Shortly after that, Ramdev met Dixit in Nasik. Ramdev agreed to sell Dixit's CDs at his yoga camps for a commission, remembers Roopesh Pandey, a long-time friend of Dixit's and member of the Azadi Bachao Andolan who was present at the meeting.

That was a difficult year for Dixit, his colleagues remember. In 2004, around the time of the wedding of Dixit's younger brother Pradeep, a sensational allegation rocked the Andolan. 'Suddenly, his brother Pradeep constructed a house for thirty–forty lakh, a lot of money at the time. Everyone believed Rajeev Dixit took money belonging to the trust and gave it to his brother,' recalls Ram Bahadur Rai, a Padma Shri recipient and former news editor of *Jansatta* and close associate of the Gandhian socialist Jayaprakash Narayan. 'There was a big backlash ... Rajeev began to get isolated within his own organization.'

It was under these circumstances that Ramdev met a vulnerable Dixit, and a bond developed between the yoga teacher and the battle-weary swadeshi campaigner and deepened over the next three years. By 2007 Dixit would become Ramdev's mentor and a trusted aide guiding his political ambitions.

11

The Old Mentor Exits

Haridwar, 2003–05

Fame, success and money brought its own share of troubles. The inherent differences between Ramdev and Karamveer came to the fore. Fissures that they hadn't even known existed started to deepen. 'Idealism is easy when you have nothing,' says Karamveer. 'It's what you do when you have fame, money or power that matters. As a sadhu, it is even more important that it must not influence you ... Unfortunately, I saw it changing them.'

Those closest to Ramdev say he wasted no time monetizing his new-found fame. The yoga camps stopped being really free. The closer you wanted to sit to the stage at the camp, the more you had to pay. People who attended the camp for free were accommodated in the furthest enclosure from the stage. In time, the tickets also became costlier. Karamveer says this troubled him: 'We had vowed to serve people selflessly, taking only what they offered so we could continue offering services to others.' Remember, when Ramdev first came to stay with Karamveer in Haridwar the latter had two conditions to take him on as his protégé, and Ramdev had committed to a life of celibacy and to serve people for free, without seeking payment for his work.

But Madhav Kant Mishra, the brains behind Aastha, offers another point of view: 'I did not mind it because he had single-handedly revived yoga in the country. In parks, in homes, every morning people were up and about, doing yoga ... he may not have invented yoga, but he certainly popularized it. People all around the world were crazy about yoga and they were coming in droves. In the morning, if you walked down any mohalla [neighbourhood], you could hear his voice floating out of open windows. In bazaars, offices and on trains, people would vigorously rub the fingernails of one hand against the other's in the hope of turning grey hair black ... He took advantage of his popularity. Anyone would have.'

Ramdev's attachment to his family was also becoming increasingly apparent. As mentioned earlier, shortly after Ramdev set up the Divya Yog Mandir Trust, his mother, sister and younger brother came to live with him. By 2003 except for his elder brother, Devdutt, who still

The Old Mentor Exits

lives in their ancestral village, his entire family – his mother, father, younger brother and sister-in-law, sister and brother-in-law – were settled in Haridwar and actively involved with Kripalu Bagh Ashram and Diya Yog Mandir Trust. His father still helps out in Ramdev's business empire and, as mentioned earlier, Ram Bharat plays a major role as controller of the cash and finances.

This may not seem odd to a layperson but it is an egregious violation of the holy oaths Ramdev had taken, including the condition of forsaking his family. Remember, Ramdev was compelled to accept saffron robes from Shankar Dev – and take these oaths – in order to be able to inherit Kripalu Bagh Ashram.

All this deeply troubled Karamveer, who believed a sadhu's life was to give, not take. He believed that there should have been no place for moneymaking and self-interest in Ramdev's life. 'I saw the idealism slipping away,' he says.

Then, sometime in the years 2003–04, according to Karamveer and several other Haridwar residents, Ramdev bought a bike and a house for his younger brother, Ram Bharat, using funds from the trust. He also bought a house for his sister and her husband, Yashdev Shastri, in Vidya Vihar Colony in Kankhal, Haridwar. Karamveer recalls how much this had bothered Balkrishna at that time. Prone to insecurity and ambition in equal measure, Balkrishna may have been jealous of Ramdev's ascendancy and upset at his own relative unimportance. But, Karamveer says, 'Balkrishna was still holding on to his ideals. Since he was closer to me at that time, as I had mentored him for longer, he came to me ... I counselled him to let it go, but Balkrishna was adamant.'

Yet, the temperamental Balkrishna was not the only one who was upset. Others in Kankhal recall what they call the 'bhai-bhatijaization' of the trust and Karamveer's disdain of it. He openly used to say, 'This money belongs to the trust and is for public good. Why was it handed over to any one individual?' According to Dr Veena Shastri, the trust was being commercialized and turned into a business.

From this point on the differences only sharpened. Early one morning, Karamveer confronted Ramdev. This is his version of their conversation:

'Until yesterday, you protested against family members getting too involved with the life of sadhus. When a sadhu brings in his family, the ashram gets lost to the family. Today what are you doing?' Karamveer demanded an explanation.

Ramdev refused to engage in a debate and told Karamveer, 'The conditions in my village are very bad. There is no water. I am sorry, but I cannot abandon my family.'

The Old Mentor Exits

'Then you should not have become a sadhu,' Karamveer replied.

'I don't want to argue with you. You do not understand. I *became* a sadhu for my family. I cannot leave them.'

'Then *I* will have to leave you.'

Karamveer told their guru Shankar Dev about this exchange. 'He felt betrayed and heartbroken. "This is very, very wrong," he had said,' recalls Karamveer.

The year 2004 had nearly drawn to a close. And so had Karamveer's part in the tale of Ramdev's rise – he had helped Ramdev acquire an ashram, taught him how to teach yoga and now there was nothing more for him to offer his protégé who was striking out on his own. Besides, a new mentor was making his mark on Ramdev's life: the swadeshi activist Rajeev Dixit who would help Ramdev sculpt his politics and economic worldview.

On Friday, 25 March 2005, the day of Holi, Karamveer quietly and without telling anyone left Kripalu Bagh Ashram in a car, never to return. He got off at Roorkee and sent the car and his mobile phone back with the driver.

It is not clear how Balkrishna's unease with Ramdev's conduct was finally resolved or what understanding they came to. Many years of shared history have locked the two men together, and neither can break free easily. Balkrishna and Ramdev simply know too much about each other. Perhaps Balkrishna's ambition left him hanging on to the coat-tails of Ramdev. In exchange for burying the hatchet and soldiering on, Ramdev eventually rewarded Balkrishna's ambitions. When the time was right, Ramdev lent his vassal fame, at the helm of his yet-to-be-born empire.

12

The Seeds of an Empire

Haridwar, 2005

Ramdev seized every opportunity to expand and grow. Tarun Kumar, Ramdev's neighbour who often took morning walks down the canal with Karamveer and Ramdev, says, 'I was only a teenager, but even I'd noticed Ramdev take every chance to meet visiting dignitaries, be it politicians, religious gurus, businessmen. He'd meet them, attend to them, build a bond . . . that is after all how people become big. He was really good at seeing an opportunity.'

Ramdev's instinct was leading him to dream bigger and wilder dreams. Politicians such as Mulayam Singh Yadav had approached him with proposals to set up his clinics in the hundred townships that the Uttar Pradesh government was planning to build at the time. Even though that plan did not get off the drawing board, his relationship with chief ministers Mulayam Singh Yadav and Narayan Dutt Tiwari continued to deepen. It ensured minimal government interference in his expansion plans and made government permissions easy to come by.

Around this time, Ramdev's friendship with Subrata Roy – who would go on to be sentenced to jail by the Supreme Court in August 2012 for defrauding three crore investors of Rs 17,400 crore through a Ponzi scheme – was also solidifying. A visible sign of those deepening ties was that Subrata Roy's financial adviser O.P. Srivastava began advising Ramdev and Balkrishna on how to manage and invest their new wealth. Kankhal residents remember Srivastava often arriving in Haridwar to hand-hold his new friends as they made their first land purchases. Srivastava's wife, Renu, tied a rakhi on Ramdev's wrist – symbolic of them treating each other as brother and sister. This further cemented the bond between the two men.

One of their key early decisions under Srivastava's watch was to found a new trust, Patanjali Yogpeeth. A number of factors may have triggered the decision to create a new trust: the rift with Karamveer who was vice-president of the Divya Yog Mandir Trust, the fact that there were too many trustees on the earlier trust, or the fact that their benefactor and convener of the

The Seeds of an Empire

Divya Yog Mandir Trust, Shankar Dev, was becoming increasingly withdrawn and taciturn. It may also have been that, having already run into trouble with the sales tax authorities, Ramdev and Balkrishna wanted to start afresh, on a clean slate. It may even have been that their new political friends wanted to do business only with them and did not care for the strings attached to the old trust.

So on 4 February 2005 Ramdev and Balkrishna founded Patanjali Yogpeeth. They were no longer willing to be fettered by old allies. The future was here, their plans were ready and they were ready to strike out alone, co-owners of a shared empire.

Srivastava also brought in other businessmen to explore the possibility of alliances, collaboration and investment, according to Sunil Pandey, a lifelong resident of Haridwar and long-time reporter at *Jansatta* who wrote about Ramdev's rise as it was unfolding.

Ramdev and Balkrishna also began buying land down the river from their Kankhal ashram, just off an arterial highway connecting the national capital of Delhi to the religious capital of Haridwar. Here, construction began for their ambitious 200-bed Ayurvedic hospital and college.

~

Delhi, 2004

The wheel of fortune was not only turning in favour of Ramdev and Balkrishna. Earlier, in May 2004, in New Delhi, the Congress returned to power after eight years when the Bharatiya Janata Party (BJP) government was voted out, further consolidating Ramdev's loyalties with Congress leader N.D. Tiwari and party ally in Uttar Pradesh Mulayam Singh Yadav.

Two months after the Congress-led UPA government was sworn in, Subodh Kant Sahay, minister of state for food processing industries, announced in New Delhi that a comprehensive law was going to be formulated for a single regulatory authority for the food processing industry. Until then, the food processing industry was a harrowing maze of regulations, governed by eight different laws and orders: the Vegetable Oil Products (Control) Order 1947, the Prevention of Food Adulteration Act 1954, the Fruit Products Order 1955, the Essential Commodities Act 1955 (in relation to food), the Solvent Extracted Oil, De-oiled Meal and Edible Flour (Control) Order 1967, the Meat Food Products Order 1973, the Milk and Milk Products Order 1992 and the Edible Oils Packaging (Regulation) Order 1998.

Under the proposed new Food Safety and Standards Act, the government would overhaul all eight laws and orders and bring Indian food processing up to international standards – including by introducing legislation on packaging and labelling.

'Given the potential of India to feed the world, it was necessary to create a regulatory framework that would allow Indian entrepreneurs to compete effectively. We planned to set up five hundred food parks to ensure higher growth,' says Sahay. The government promised a grant of Rs 50 crore to entrepreneurs to set up the infrastructure for these parks for food processing.

Sahay's policy initiative found its way into India's Eleventh Five Year Plan (2007–12) as a specific goal for the ministry of food processing industries: to set up a food park in every state. The first phase would involve construction of ten food parks, including in Uttar Pradesh and Uttarakhand.

Even Sahay did not know then that he was sowing the seeds of Ramdev's FMCG empire and Patanjali's food business.

~

Mumbai, end 2005

Even though Aastha's owners were in trouble with SEBI, Ramdev had become a sensation. Millions were listening to every word he uttered each morning, as he exhorted them to believe in themselves, believe that they could be well again through pranayama and yoga alone, believe that they could be rid of allopathic doctors and their medicines. It surprised no one that from the love and adulation of his followers flowed seemingly inexhaustible wealth.

Within three years of his first televised appearance on Aastha in 2003, Ramdev's empire – whose assets included the Divya Pharmacy building, Patanjali Yogpeeth I that housed his Ayurvedic hospital and college, and Patanjali Yogpeeth II that housed a nursery for growing medicinal herbs – was worth about Rs 100 crore. Money poured in every week in the form of donations from well-wishers and followers.

In January 2006 the *Tribune* newspaper wrote about how, buoyed by continuing western interest in yoga, people all around the country were taking it up and yoga gurus were 'raking in fame and fortune'. Ramdev's name led the rest. Comparing his Bangalore yoga camp (7800 people attended it) to a Shah Rukh Khan live programme, the report claimed that tickets to Ramdev's camp cost between Rs 500 and Rs 2100, and so Ramdev was estimated to have made 'a cool Rs 75-80 lakhs' at the seven-day camp. His Nasik camp in December 2005 reportedly mopped up Rs 3 crore.

Aastha, meanwhile, devotedly live-cast his camps.

The Seeds of an Empire

Towards the end of 2005 Krishna Kumar Pittie, an admiring Marwari businessman who traded and manufactured commodities such as silver and steel and dabbled in real estate, organized a hugely successful yog vigyan shivir for Ramdev in Mumbai. The Pitties financed, organized and managed the entire event in the business district of Bandra Kurla Complex. Its proceeds, estimated to be around Rs 4–5 crore by Pittie, were donated entirely to Ramdev. 'I knew it would be successful but even I was blown away when 40,000 people came in the morning and another 40–50,000 people came in the evening,' says Pittie, who went on to become a key distributor for Patanjali products.

During the camp, Mumbai celebrities and socialites, musicians and businessmen – including Bollywood actors Anil Kapoor, Shekhar Suman, Mallika Sherawat, Hema Malini and even the classical flutist Pandit Hariprasad Chaurasia – all made a beeline to pay their respects to the emerging yoga guru. Shortly after this, Ramdev would even coach Amitabh Bachchan and his son, Abhishek, in yoga and pranayama.

'No one came without a donation. Most of his Mumbai meetings during those days used to happen at my house. He never met anyone for free,' says Kirit Mehta. 'Some gave Rs 1 lakh, some gave two. But no one ever came empty-handed.'

'Even those who could not afford it wanted to contribute... because everyone benefited from his yoga and pranayama in some way or the other,' says Pittie.

By this time, lifetime membership to Baba Ramdev's yoga centre in Haridwar carried a price tag of Rs 1 lakh. For a 'patron membership', people had to fork out Rs 2.5 lakh.

13

Enter Brinda Karat

Haridwar, 2005–06

Ramdev and Balkrishna's enterprise was thriving and expanding. Trucks filled with packaged and labelled Ayurvedic medicines rolled out ceaselessly, bound for stores across the country.

But trouble wasn't far behind.

Not long after Karamveer left the ashram in March 2005, there were huge lay-offs – 113 of 400 workers of the pharmacy were sacked. These were mostly women who received about Rs 1200 in wages every month. The statutory minimum wage in the state was Rs 1740 at that time. The trigger for the sacking was that the workers went on an indefinite strike. They were demanding official letters of appointment, the wages that were lawfully due to them and benefits of the provident fund and the employees state insurance schemes.

Until then, friends and family ran much of their enterprise. Balkrishna and Ramdev, still relatively new to playing the role of formal employers on such a scale, failed to see the strike as an opportunity to build goodwill or share some of their good fortune with others. Instead they saw it as a threat and in response fired the striking workers. It was clear that they wanted to make an example of them to ensure that such a thing did not happen again and to send out a clear signal that they were not going to get bullied.

Not unexpectedly, the workers turned for help to the Centre of Indian Trade Unions (CITU), a union politically affiliated with the Communist Party of India (Marxist), or CPI(M). The workers, including the vocal Sushma Mishra, Chandra Pal Dubey and Ratan Pal Singh, lodged a complaint under the Industrial Disputes Act with the deputy labour commissioner, government of Uttarakhand. CITU, with its reputation for fiercely protecting workers' rights, was a formidable opponent for Ramdev.

To diffuse tensions, Divya Pharmacy management representatives attended a tripartite meeting with the workers and district administration to resolve the issue on 21 May 2005. In an article published on 15 January 2006 in *People's Democracy*, the weekly newspaper of the

Enter Brinda Karat

CPI(M), the CITU declared the meeting a resounding success. 'In the meeting, the management committed themselves to pay minimum wages to the workmen as per the government notification and the workers agreed to restore normalcy from May 22, 2005. The trust management agreed not to take any disciplinary action against the workers.'

That should have been the end of the affair. But the following morning, the management did not allow the workers to return to work. Instead, the article in *People's Democracy* claims, 'they implicated 46 workers in fictitious police cases'. The agreement was never implemented and the workers were never reinstated.

But what Ramdev's team did not know was that while exiting, some of these workers had procured samples of two medicines – Kuliya bhasm, a drug to treat epilepsy, and Yaunamritbati, a drug to cure impotence – from Ramdev's hospital, Brahmakalp Chikitsalay, in Haridwar as well as some ingredients from the pharmacy's manufacturing unit.

The workers went to the CPI(M) leader Brinda Karat with these items. According to Karat, what the workers brought to her were 'the testicle of some sort of wildcat'. She continues: 'They told me this is what was imported from Afghanistan and put into the medicines. They also told me that deer horns and crushed human skulls were regularly used in their medicines. I was horrified not because these things were used. I was horrified because there was no mention of these things on the ingredient lists.'

~

On 3 January 2006 Brinda Karat brought serious allegations against Ramdev and the Divya Yog Pharmacy. Backed by a letter from Shiv Basant, then a joint secretary in the health ministry, she accused Ramdev of adulteration – specifically, of adding human and animal bones in his medicines – and labelling violations.

Earlier, the medicine samples procured by the agitating workers had been passed from one government office to the next. When the principal secretary, health, of Uttaranchal, Sujit Das, refused to take the samples for testing, as the state did not have the requisite facilities for this, the samples were sent to the Union health ministry. From there, they travelled to the department of Ayurveda, yoga, naturopathy, unani, siddha and homeopathy (AYUSH).

In December 2005 AYUSH released the findings of its lab tests. They had found traces of human and animal DNA in the samples. The final report said that Ayurveda allowed the use of these materials, but the pharmacy was in violation of licensing and labelling laws under the Indian Drugs and Cosmetics Act, 1940.

Enter Brinda Karat

Karat also accused Divya Yog Pharmacy of not honouring the tripartite agreement to re-employ the 113 sacked workers and pay them the minimum wage that was due to them.

The first set of charges, those to do with adulteration and mislabelling, were very serious indeed. If proved they could have resulted in jail time for Ramdev.

But Ramdev, ever the skilful smooth talker, and master of theatre, successfully managed to turn the issue on its head. He did not address the allegations of the sacked workers at all, and instead claimed that the samples of Divya Pharmacy's medicines and ingredients had been deliberately tampered with. He attacked Karat and accused her of colluding with 'foreign companies' to attack not just him but yoga and Ayurveda itself. In a brilliant sleight of hand, Ramdev made himself synonymous with these great Indian traditions. Karat was painted as the disbelieving communist conspiring to tarnish India's great heritage by attacking him. Ramdev had a huge advantage that Karat did not: he could marshal Rajeev Dixit's vocabulary and plank of swadeshi, he could invoke hurt Hindu pride and sentiment, and he could speak directly to millions of television viewers via Aastha. Ramdev portrayed Karat as a stooge of multinational companies that peddle colas, pizzas and expensive treatments.

Ramdev's recasting of the issue – and the media's

willingness to play along – worked like a charm. Karat's charges of wrongdoing were instantly forgotten. Instead, she found herself vilified, in the eye of a political maelstrom. A curious coalition of politicians from across the country – the BJP, Shiv Sena, Nationalist Congress Party, Samajwadi Party (Mulayam Singh Yadav) and Rashtriya Janata Dal (Lalu Prasad Yadav) – coalesced around Ramdev and extended him their unqualified support.

Brinda Karat believes that the case was deliberately mishandled by the political brass, mainly because Ramdev's powerful friends did not want any harm to come to him. During an interview with *Frontline* magazine in 2013, Karat said, 'Instead of looking at the facts of the case the assumption was that a person who had so many followers was automatically above any wrongdoing ... [B]ecause the then Chief Minister, who was a Congressman, was himself taking medicines from Ramdev, even a police report by worker-witnesses was not allowed to be filed. So, instead of an investigation, what happened was a massive cover-up and permanent destruction of all evidence to ensure that there could be no case even in the future.'

Recounting her meeting with the then Congress chief minister, N.D. Tiwari, Karat says, 'I had gone to appeal to him to please allow the police to question the workers and take their testimony about the ingredients

Enter Brinda Karat

put in his medicines. He flatly refused to do that. He told me, "I will do anything you ask for the workers. But please don't ask me to do anything against Ramdev. I will not be able to do it.'"

It was a clear signal of Ramdev's clout in the ruling Congress party that a sitting chief minister had no trouble admitting that Ramdev could not be touched. This is especially telling given that Karat's CPM was no ordinary party at that time. The UPA government's smooth survival depended on the support it was getting from the communists.

Ramdev has a natural talent for reading the pulse of the people and a flair for showmanship and giving people what they want. And so when the Shriram Institute of Industrial Research laboratory later gave his medicine samples a clean chit, instead of letting the issue die, he pressed his advantage. Ramdev had turned Karat's attack on him into a sensational and high-visibility opportunity to attack multinationals, and he wasn't going to back down.

Ramdev, the outsider with a clean image, realized that his constituency of believers and the ready stage that Aastha channel provided him made him powerful enough to take on people high up in the establishment.

The incident was a warning to political leaders. Ramdev was no ordinary yoga teacher. He was a political force with a pan-Indian constituency. As politicians across the country began speaking in his defence, it was difficult not to speculate: Were parties pledging allegiance to Ramdev because they were also sensing an opportunity for a political alliance? Were they thinking: Stay on his right side today and he can swing voters for you tomorrow?

14

Patanjali Is Born

Haridwar, 13 January 2006

Ten days after Brinda Karat's allegations, while Ramdev was still engaged in a messy public battle with her, Balkrishna incorporated and registered a new company – Patanjali Ayurveda Private Limited – with the objective to 'carry on the business of manufacture, process, refine, formulate, import, export, buy, sell and otherwise deal in all kinds of pharmaceutical products, ayurvedic, unani, homeopathic, allopathic medicines and herbal cosmetics, herbal and life saving drugs'. Patanjali Ayurveda had an authorized share capital of Rs 10 lakh that was divided into one lakh shares of Rs 10 each. Acharya Balkrishna held 90,000 shares and Swami Muktananda, a close aide, held 10,000 shares. But over the years this shareholding structure would change several times. The only constant is that Balkrishna, Ramdev's controllable deputy, is and was always the largest shareholder by miles. As mentioned earlier, it would have caused a scandal for a renunciate to have shares in his or his family members' names.

The formation of the company signalled Ramdev and Balkrishna's readiness to break away from the limitations of the structure of a trust. They were ready to work towards the clear goal of earning profits for its shareholders. During the course of the year, five other companies would be incorporated by Balkrishna. Some of them still exist; others have been closed down. The year 2006 marked the beginning of a company-formation spree and over the following decade Balkrishna would serve as director of no fewer than thirty-seven companies.

But the company at the centre of Ramdev's story and the one destined for fabulous success was Patanjali Ayurveda.

When the ministry of food processing industries began accepting applications for its food park scheme, Ramdev and Balkrishna wasted no time in sending their proposal. Patanjali Ayurveda quickly received the necessary approvals to set up a food park in Uttarakhand.

15

The Yoga Roadshow

London, July 2006

Kirit Mehta had watched Ramdev take the country by storm and command the hearts of millions around the world. As the owner of Aastha International, which beamed Aastha India's content to the United Kingdom and the United States, Mehta had a global audience he needed to take care of and nurture. So he decided to nudge Ramdev to take a global tour.

Bhakti Mehta, Kirit's daughter, remembers: 'I was present during that conversation between Ramdev and my father. My father told him that there are our people there as well who need you.' Bhakti was closely involved with the business then and now runs another religious channel in the United Arab Emirates. 'At that time he [Ramdev] would do whatever my father told him to.'

Ramdev had never been abroad and so passports were prepared for him and his team. The Mehtas also helped Ramdev and his team of forty secure visas. 'He could not have done that camp without us. In England, we held yoga shivirs in Leicester, Coventry, Manchester and Harrow,' says Kirit Mehta.

Ramdev's foreign tour was a bigger success than any of them had imagined in their wildest dreams. At a small ceremony in a House of Commons committee room, Ramdev was given the 'Mahaveer Award' by an Indian organization for his contribution towards the promotion of Indian culture and values. One can only imagine how he felt when, within a month of getting his first passport, he found himself in the gardens of Buckingham Palace at a tea party hosted by Queen Elizabeth.

Soon after the palace garden party and his successful yoga camps in the UK Ramdev addressed, at the invitation of the United Nations secretary general, political leaders from 150 nations gathered in New York for a conference on poverty alleviation.

But those camps in the UK also brought out a darker side of Ramdev. According to Bhakti Mehta, she saw Ramdev's men tampering with the scales before and after the event to give people a sense that they had lost more weight than they actually had. At the end of the camps, Ramdev encouraged people to share their new body weight. 'When some simpler people made some outrageous weight-loss claim, Ramdev would call that person to speak to the camera and egg him on. Excited by the cameras trained on them, people would say they'd lost unbelievable amounts of weight . . . later, these people, Ramdev and his cronies, would all laugh at the man,' Bhakti recalls.

But Ramdev fudging yoga camp weight-loss results was not the only thing the Mehtas observed that summer. 'We saw how money-hungry, power-hungry he really was,' Bhakti says. According to Bhakti, who organized the event, tickets cost GBP 500. Then at the end of each day of the shivirs, Ramdev visited homes of people who made donations of GBP 11,000 for the honour of hosting him. It was during these visits that Bhakti asserts they saw some troubling things. 'It was common practice for hosts to place a large, stretched cloth under the sofa by his feet,' she says. Visitors, friends and family of the hosts would come and touch his feet, and when they emerged from the nosedive, there would be notes – pounds and dollars – at Ramdev's feet. At the end of a meet-and-greet, 'his two assistants . . . rolled it [the cloth with the offerings] up into a ball, tossed it in the car. He made his men sit every night – check every note, check every counterfoil, count it all the very same night. It was really important to him to know how much he had brought in every night and, for the first time, we saw how attached he really was to his money,' Bhakti recalls.

Ramdev and his team returned home, mopping up two million pounds – about Rs 17 crore at the then prevalent exchange rate of Rs 85 to a pound, according to the Mehtas. It is not clear if the money was repatriated back to India or left behind in the Patanjali Yogpeeth Trust that Ramdev formed in the UK during that trip.

~

Ramdev was beginning to understand how powerful he was. He was well aware of the influence he wielded thanks to his army of supporters. He was also clear-eyed about how reliant Aastha now was on his star power – not the other way around. He wanted to control the medium himself, and not in the least be fettered by its owners.

And so a plan was cooked up: three months after their return from London, in October 2006, Balkrishna and Muktananda, directors of one Swami Healthcare Pvt. Ltd, changed the company's name to Vedic Aarogya Pvt. Ltd. The new memorandum of association changed the company's defined objectives to include 'information and technology, telecommunication, satellite, internet, networking etc.' activities.

Clearly, Ramdev was taking preparatory steps to become a media house owner.

According to a notice filed by the company at the Registrar of Companies, on 21 May 2007, an extraordinary meeting of the shareholders (i.e., Acharya Balkrishna and Swami Muktananda) was held at the registered office of the company (i.e., Kripalu Bagh Ashram, where both of them lived and worked). During that meeting the stated objectives of the company were altered, making their intention even clearer: 'To undertake, carry on and conduct the business of proprietors and operators of Television stations, Radio broadcasting, transmitting and receiving stations, News channels, religious and educational channels, health channels and any other stations used for visual and/or sound transmissions or reception by any other contrivance or means whatsoever.'

The next day, on 22 May 2007, the company changed its name again, from Vedic Aarogya Pvt. Ltd to Vedic Broadcastings Pvt. Ltd, finally dropping all pretence of being a health-care company. As with their other companies, Balkrishna was the biggest shareholder of this new company too.

With the formation of Vedic Broadcasting, Ramdev and his closest aides were ready in the wings, prepared to move in to take over Aastha.

16

Mystery 2: The Guru's Disappearance

Haridwar, June 2007

A year after Ramdev had a successful run in the United Kingdom and delivered a speech at the United Nations in New York came plans for a yoga tour of the United States. India's foremost yoga guru was scheduled to start his tour in New York on 30 June 2007 and wind it up in Coventry in the UK on 8 August, rumbling through New Jersey, Chicago, Glasgow and London in between.

Animesh Goenka, then president of Heritage India, a small charitable organization that was involved with the planning of Ramdev's tour, had told the media that the US leg of the tour, estimated to cost $350,000, was to be funded exclusively through charitable donations from private individuals and corporations. The sale of tickets to the yoga camps, priced between $100 and $500, was expected to raise half a million dollars. This money, Goenka had asserted, would be funnelled into research on amla and developing a product for which a patent could be sought.

While Ramdev prepared for his international tour, Balkrishna was making certain critical and far-reaching changes. On 18 May 2007, fifteen months after its formation, Patanjali Ayurveda Pvt. Ltd dropped the word 'private' from its name. This was a critical move if the company wanted to list itself on the stock market. Patanjali's shareholding also changed around this time, as would happen frequently over the years, with several of Ramdev's key associates coming on board as shareholders, albeit minor ones, at this point. As before, and as with Vedic Broadcasting Pvt. Ltd, Ramdev's pliant and trustworthy Balkrishna remained the largest shareholder by far.

Notable among these new shareholders were Krishan Kumar Pittie and Sarvan Poddar. Pittie would eventually play a major role in Ramdev's quest for media domination and Poddar would buy a Scottish island, Little Cumbrae, for GBP 2.1 million in September 2009 and donate it to Patanjali Yogpeeth's UK trust.

Balkrishna also converted Vedic Broadcasting Pvt. Ltd into a public limited company.

Kirit Mehta and his partners at Aastha were too busy

Mystery 2: The Guru's Disappearance

struggling to survive to notice the dramatic changes that were taking place in Vedic Broadcasting's story. Had they been a little more alert they would have sensed that something wasn't quite sitting right. Ramdev was preparing to take over Aastha.

But Ramdev himself missed something brewing in his own backyard. Amid his heady successes, and hectic travel, he failed to see that his guru Shankar Dev was ailing, increasingly unhappy and isolated in his own home, Kripalu Bagh Ashram. For instance, Shankar Dev, who was the convener of the Divya Yog Mandir Trust, was not on the boards of any of the new companies that were set up by Ramdev.

But what Ramdev could not see, though it was in plain sight, many in Haridwar saw. Several remember the swiftly ageing Shankar Dev, ravaged by spinal tuberculosis, becoming increasingly frail and forlorn. Spinal tuberculosis causes the patient to cough blood, lose weight, get night sweats and chills, and experience a loss of appetite, fatigue and fever, and it can sometimes impair mobility as a result of pain in the spine and damage to the joints.

Like in many small towns, friendships and kinship survive long years in Kankhal. Sushant Mahendru's family, friends of Shankar Dev, continued looking out for him even after he stopped coming to their house when his old friend died. 'I have seen him several times during those months when he had TB. He was alone and ignored in a little room in Kripalu Bagh Ashram . . . cooking for himself, washing his own clothes and utensils. The only difference was that he took rickshaws to commute because he could no longer cycle because of the TB. But even that was difficult for him . . . These people [Ramdev and Balkrishna] had a Nissan Terrano at the time, but not one person in Kankhal has any memory of Shankar Dev sitting in any of their cars. He was always on a cycle or in a rickshaw,' says Mahendru.

The anguish of watching Shankar Dev deteriorate is etched on Mahendru's face. From being the master of his ashram, Shankar Dev was reduced to a sidestepped has-been in Kripalu Bagh.

Shankar Dev is still the subject of hushed conversations in Kankhal today. Those who remember tell of his trials and speak of his tribulations in lowered voices – no one wants to cross the now all-powerful Ramdev. In a small place like Kankhal, word can get around. They are right to be worried. For instance, when I asked about Shankar Dev's deteriorating standard of living Balkrishna became positively belligerent and furious at me.

Mystery 2: The Guru's Disappearance

Chicago, 14 July 2007

Ramdev's tour began successfully in New York when a thousand people, mostly Indian Americans already familiar with his yoga through Aastha USA, attended his inaugural camp at Nassau Community College – some from as far as California.

At the Garden State Exhibit Center in Somerset, New Jersey, there was a groundswell of fan support – 3000 people attended. The state Senate and the General Assembly passed a resolution that 'this Legislature honors Swami Ramdev for his firm belief that good health is the birthright of all human beings, and extends best wishes for a successful yoga camp in the US'.

It was when Ramdev was in Chicago that news came from Kankhal. On 14 July 2007, Shankar Dev disappeared. Vanished without a trace. He left that morning for his usual walk and simply did not return.

It may have been devastating news for Ramdev. Or maybe it was just inconvenient timing. With the Chicago schedule drawing to a close, Ramdev had to choose: Should he go on to London, where the House of Commons planned to receive and honour him, or should he send his regrets and rush back to Kankhal to lead the search for his missing guru?

Usually once a disciple takes deeksha, or initiation into the sacred, from his guru, he establishes a bond with him. Ramdev had not just taken deeksha from Shankar Dev but also accepted saffron robes from him – that is, he renounced the world. From the moment he took the saffron robes from Shankar Dev, that guru–shishya relationship was meant to become the central fulcrum of his life. From that moment onward, Ramdev was supposed to consider his guru as his spiritual and temporal father and mother.

There is no way of knowing what Ramdev truly felt when he heard of the disappearance or if he struggled with the decision or for how long, but in the end he decided to carry on with his tour. The day after his aides filed a missing person's report at Kankhal police station, on 18 July 2007, Ramdev attended a ceremony at the British House of Commons in his honour.

An investigation began in India, but clues were scarce. A cryptic note was found in Shankar Dev's room: 'I have taken some loan from you for this trust but I cannot repay it. Please forgive me. I am leaving.' He was seventy-seven years old.

The note raised more questions than it answered: Exactly how much did this old man who continued to live as simply as before Ramdev's meteoric rise borrow that he could not repay the sum? Why did he borrow it? When had he taken the loan? And from whom? More importantly – why did Ramdev, sitting atop an empire worth at least Rs 100 crore, not repay the loan

Mystery 2: The Guru's Disappearance

on his behalf? Why did Shankar Dev not ask him for help? Or had he?

Even though Karamveer had left the organization, Shankar Dev, who missed him dearly, often called him – sometimes for financial help. 'I used to send whatever little I could so he could get by,' says Karamveer. Vipin Pradhan, a former aide and Karamveer's nephew, says, 'By then, the trust was being run by . . . relatives of Ramdev who had come in from outside and had no intention of serving any interest other than their own. They treated Shankar Dev badly and he was very unhappy.'

Karamveer says that once when he was visiting Haridwar and staying with an old friend in Tripura Ashram, 'Shankar Dev came to meet me. They had sent two people after him to do his CID [that is, to spy on him]. They waited at the gates while we met. I'm not sure why . . . they [Ramdev and Balkrishna] had doubts [about Shankar Dev] in their minds at the time . . . who knows what doubt . . . what they were thinking at the time. It must have been a very difficult situation for Shankar Dev.'

But it is Radhika Nagrath's appraisal of the situation that is most damning. Remember, Nagrath is the one who designed Divya Pharmacy's website in its early days. She is still associated with Patanjali and has an obvious soft spot for Ramdev, whom she speaks of with affection, though she is unhesitatingly honest. She says, 'Shankar Dev was a real saint – a very gentle guy. He felt ousted in his own home. He did not get any compassion because these people were in a race for something else. It was once his home, his shelter. He used to sign all the expense cheques for the trust at first [but] now the authority was taken away from him and he was not happy with the way things had shaped out. He had given these people shelter and now they had no time for him . . . they had no use for an old man any more.'

An uneasy silence always follows questions about Shankar Dev among Kankhal residents. People always ask, 'Can I trust you? Are you writing for him or against him? You see, Ramdev has become too powerful. And look what happened to his guru . . .'

~

After his pit stop at the House of Commons, Ramdev continued his tour, travelling to Glasgow then back to London, and finally ending his tour in Coventry on 8 August 2007. When he returned to India, more than three weeks had passed since Shankar Dev's disappearance. To outside observers it seemed as though Ramdev was too busy chasing fame and fortune, making them wonder: did he even care?

After his return, Ramdev summoned a press

Mystery 2: The Guru's Disappearance

conference in Haridwar, remembers the *Jansatta* reporter and Haridwar resident Sunil Pandey. 'At the press conference he was saying how Shankar Dev was like a father to him and how sad it was ... I asked him that if he really was like a father to him, why didn't he come back?'

'I was in the US, conducting camps,' answered Ramdev.

'Well, if a family member disappeared, one would come back, isn't it?' Pandey pressed Ramdev.

'If I knew he was alive, I would have,' replied Ramdev.

'So you are admitting that you know that he is dead?' demanded Pandey.

That was the suspicion in everyone's minds.

Stunned, realizing he had misspoken, Ramdev fell silent.

'Then his people just took over and changed the subject. Though a lot of people were present at the press conference,' recalls Pandey.

Little of this murky business was reported in the national media at that time. Across the country, Ramdev's star was ascendant.

It was only in October 2012, five years after Shankar Dev's disappearance, that the Central Bureau of Investigation (CBI), India's apex investigative agency, initiated a probe to find him. In his inimitable style, Ramdev welcomed the investigation on the one hand, but also attacked the CBI and the government, accusing them of a politically motivated conspiracy to frame him in the case. Given the sour relationship between Ramdev and the Union government at that time, his allegation did have some credence.

Whatever the CBI's initial motivations, it was widely reported that it initiated a move to close the case in December 2014 – by this time the Narendra Modi–led government had taken charge at the Centre – because the agency had failed to make any headway. The special CBI magistrate in Dehradun set the date for the next hearing as 12 January 2015 but this is where the public case file goes cold.

It's hard to ascertain what happened thereafter. While a right to information (RTI) request I filed with the CBI in Delhi met with the response that the CBI was not covered by the RTI, another filed in Dehradun met with the response that the CBI does not answer questions on open cases. Ergo, the case is still open.

17

The Reinvention

Haridwar, 2008

Ramdev's yoga camps and tours were beginning to seem dated and were losing their appeal. He planned a 'yoga cruise' around Singapore and Halong Bay in Vietnam to liven things up, but even that did not seem enough to hold viewers.

Ramdev needed something new, a fresh hook to reel in and keep his audience.

Amid this sense of ennui and 'what next?' Ramdev was becoming closer to Rajeev Dixit. Over the past couple of years Dixit had taken to sharing the stage with Ramdev during yoga camps. His speeches had an electrifying effect on Ramdev's audiences. Ramdev must have sensed the alchemic potential of mixing his yoga with Dixit's swadeshi economics.

Rajeev Dixit himself had been feeling that his socio-economic message, powerful as it was, was not reaching enough people. Additionally, as mentioned earlier, his alleged misappropriation of funds had led to an estrangement of sorts with his organization, the Azadi Bachao Andolan. Disillusioned with the major political parties, and isolated in his organization, he was hunting for a platform to take his campaign against black money and multinational companies in India to the next level.

In 2008 this search brought Dixit to Pranav Pandya, leader of the Gayatri Pariwar in Haridwar, whose global following exceeded 90 million followers. 'But I had to tell him that I am an apolitical man and my followers would not want me to launch political parties,' says Pandya.

While Pandya rebuffed Dixit, Ramdev courted him. Ramdev's political ambitions were surging. By 2007–08 Ramdev 'felt that yoga alone had reached its maximum potential and that swadeshi could help him expand his sphere of influence . . . but Ramdev also believed that he did not have the capacity to do what Rajeev Dixit was doing alone,' says Pradeep Dixit, Rajeev's younger brother. 'He needed my brother. My brother needed a platform, which Ramdev offered in the form of the channel Aastha.'

Two men, one with a message, the other with a medium, began plotting a revolution through their new national grassroots movement – Bharat Swabhiman Andolan – which they hoped would grow into a political party over the next few years, and maybe even become powerful enough to contest the 2014 general elections.

Dixit was now shaping Ramdev's political-economic messaging. I had witnessed Dixit discuss swadeshi economics with Ramdev on the porch steps of Ramdev's cottage in Yog Gram, a yoga and Ayurvedic retreat established by him in Haridwar, while reporting a story for *Mint* in 2008. Ahead of the 2009 general elections, Ramdev's political ambition was guarded, yet palpable.

Ramdev spelt out his goal during our interview in late July 2008. A year later he would launch his first political yatra in September 2009. Ramdev had declared then his intention to field candidates in every constituency in the country in the 2014 elections. 'My mission is to remind Indians of who they are, their heritage and be proud of it. By next year, my Bharat Swabhiman Andolan will have reached 50 crore people. And then, there will be a revolution,' Ramdev had said.

Within months an opportunity to lead a political movement presented itself.

The Vishwa Hindu Parishad (VHP), buoyed by their successful campaign to protect the Ram Setu in 2007, had set their sights on protecting the river Ganga. Ahead of the 2009 national elections, the issue was ripe for political picking. Ashok Tripathi, the then president of the Ganga Mahasabha, an organization working to preserve and protect the river, recollects: 'Under the leadership of the VHP president Ashok Singhal, Hindu organizations were all coming together to demand two things – that the Ganga be called a national river, and that it be made free of all checks and dams.' To this end, a meeting was called in Haridwar.

Ramdev, quick to see an opportunity, hurried to offer his stage – the Patanjali Yogpeeth and Aastha channel – to rouse mass support for the movement. 'We met in June 2008. All the stakeholders, representatives of the Hindu communities, leaders, scientists and conservationists were there at the meeting. It went on for three and a half hours. He [Ramdev] spoke for most of the time from the dais and became the self-appointed convener of the Ganga Raksha Manch,' recollects Ashok Tripathi who witnessed that meeting. 'I remember telling Ashok Singhal at the end of that meeting – Baba Ramdev has just hijacked your movement.'

Tripathi was right. Viewers watching national Hindu leaders gathered in Patanjali Yogpeeth listened to Ramdev speak about the need for a movement to protect the Ganga on Aastha channel, synonymous with Ramdev. It looked as though he was the creator and leader of the campaign.

The Ganga movement galvanized hundreds of thousands of people. Ramdev showed his political canniness by focusing only on declaring the Ganga a national river, and not on the demand to free it of dams, for which it would have been much harder to get the government on board.

In November 2008 Ramdev met Prime Minister Manmohan Singh and brokered a deal: the government agreed to declare the Ganga a national river. Of course, the issue of checks and dams was relegated to the back burner and never mentioned. Ramdev had achieved his first political victory.

Thanks to Ramdev, this was also a win of sorts for the VHP-battered Congress. The ruling party had already lost ground with Hindus on the Ram Setu issue the year before. Now, with Ramdev's aid, they had not only diffused another ballooning issue, but also managed to score some brownie points with an irate community.

Ramdev was in a rare position of having friends on both sides of the aisle. He was now planning his next move.

18

The Aastha Takeover

Haridwar, November 2009

As Ramdev expanded their presence in the public space, foraying successfully into politics, Acharya Balkrishna was consolidating that expansion. In February 2009 Patanjali Ayurveda began constructing the 95-acre Patanjali Food and Herbal Park on the outskirts of Haridwar.

Another major game was afoot at this time: the takeover of Aastha TV. But first some background: When, in its final order on the Aastha case, in January 2007, SEBI permanently froze 93 per cent of Aastha's shares from being sold, making them totally worthless, and prohibited Aastha from raising money on the capital markets, Ramdev had come to a dejected Kirit Mehta's aid. According to a bitter and broken Mehta, now wheelchair-bound, his body ravaged by a stroke, Ramdev had offered to buy – through Vedic Broadcasting – a significant portion of his shares that could still be traded. Remember, only 93 per cent of Aastha's shares were frozen, the other 7 per cent could still be bought and sold. Ramdev, says Mehta, reasoned that if he were to come on board as a major shareholder, it would be easier for him to lobby government officials and judges to help Aastha out. The officialdom, Mehta claims Ramdev told him, would be softer and more amenable to offering Aastha some relief if Ramdev was seen as a major player in the channel. And so, Mehta asserts, Ramdev offered and he agreed that for the sake of appearances Ramdev would incrementally and over a period of time buy a sizeable portion of Mehta's non-frozen shares for Rs 10 crore.

In the meantime, Mehta still owned and ran Aastha International, which in turn owned Aastha USA and Aastha UK. As mentioned earlier, Aastha International was broadcasting Aastha India's content on its American and British channels – though, apparently, no formal paperwork was done granting Aastha International this right. Since Mehta was the chairman and managing director of, and the main force behind, Aastha India, this didn't seem necessary to him at that time – maybe he did not see the point of funnelling his own money through Aastha International, a solely owned company, into one that was also owned by him, albeit not entirely, and one that was also in trouble with the law.

Around that time Mehta was putting all his energy into growing and nurturing Aastha International. According to him, since he had been spending an increasing amount of time in the US and UK on Aastha International work, his second-in-command, Pramod Joshi, liaised with Ramdev. In his absence, Ramdev also became close to Hiren Doshi, the broker who was a minor shareholder in Aastha India, and the legal and commercial brains behind the company's formation. Ramdev's increasing interaction with Doshi was ostensibly because of the complex and multistaged sale of shares between him and Mehta. But Mehta darkly alleges that Ramdev gleaned much intelligence about him and his businesses through Joshi, Doshi and S.K. Jain, the other major shareholder in Aastha India, and managed to 'get them to turn against me'. An alliance, he asserts, was formed against him in Haridwar.

According to Mehta, given the multistage share transfer that was taking place between Ramdev and him, and given that he was spending much time abroad, he had left several undated, signed and unsigned, share transfer documents in his office. These, he alleges, found their way into Ramdev's hands, and were used to transfer his shares to Vedic Broadcasting Ltd; in some instances, his signature was even forged on the documents. Mehta says no consideration was paid on these transfers that were done behind his back. He adds that he wasn't even paid the agreed market price for the shares that were legitimately transferred to Vedic Broadcasting.

When Mehta found out about what was going on, he was predictably furious and demanded payment for his shares. Around this time Mehta also decided to sell the rights to broadcast Aastha India's content to the highest bidder in the US and UK. As mentioned, these rights were being exercised by Mehta's company Aastha International till then. This, Mehta alleges, Ramdev was dead against since he wanted to keep Aastha's UK and US rights within his reach.

When Pramod Joshi, Hiren Doshi and S.K. Jain caught wind of Mehta's plan to sell the international rights, they asked him to go to Haridwar with them, on the pretext that they would get Ramdev to clear all payments that he owed Mehta.

A meeting was set up in Patanjali Yogpeeth I on 15 November 2009, according to Mehta. He got on a plane with his son Chetan, Joshi and Doshi. Jain flew in from Kolkata. 'All three of them were instrumental in bringing me to Haridwar, ostensibly to discuss accounts with Ramdev. Otherwise, I would not have gone.'

As the lot of them entered Ramdev's room on the first

floor of Patanjali Yogpeeth I, where Ramdev was waiting with Balkrishna, Mehta says he sensed an immediate chill. Something had shifted and Mehta realized he had no allies in the room. Mehta says Ramdev, paranoid about secret recordings, asked to see his pen to check if it had a hidden camera. Then 'Ramdev was in full rudra swaroop ... furious, livid at me. He was screaming ... shouting ... beside himself with rage that I could even think of selling the international rights of Aastha,' recollects Mehta.

Next Ramdev made a curt demand: 'Please tender your resignation [as chairman and managing director of Aastha India] right now.' A resignation letter dated 13 November 2009 was put before Mehta as Ramdev commanded him to sign it, Mehta recollects.

Mehta had come to Haridwar to collect the money he says was due to him. But here he was being deprived of the little power and control he had over Aastha India. According to Chetan, 'Dad just stood there, not saying yes, not saying no. I kept urging him not to sign anything. I could see fear in his eyes.'

Mehta says, helpless and fearful, he ultimately signed the document. 'I was crying over there ... and I've not stopped crying inside. A man I created! How can someone do such a thing?' Kirit Mehta now had no power in Aastha. He had lost most of his shares in the company and his place as CMD. It was all over for him.

Mehta still owned Aastha International, and the TV channels Aastha UK and Aastha US. But since there had been no formal agreement allowing Aastha International to broadcast the content of Aastha India, those rights were still technically held by Aastha India. Mehta could only have sold them in his capacity as CMD of Aastha India. Now, by removing Mehta, Ramdev had ensured that the international rights would not, in fact, be sold.

According to Mehta's daughter Bhakti, within days of this, Ramdev's people took over Aastha's website, and email addresses and cut off the Mehtas' access to the company and its employees.

Just two days after that fateful meeting, fearing for their lives, the Mehta family fled to Dubai on 17 November 2009. They decided to carry on their fight from there and continued to broadcast Aastha India's content as usual on their US and UK channels. But since Aastha India technically owned these rights, Ramdev's advisers filed cases accusing the Mehtas of piracy in the UK and US.

'He [Ramdev] knew . . . that everything he had achieved was because of Aastha – the channel that gave him the power to talk to two crore viewers every day,' says Mehta. 'He wanted me to simply hand over the channel . . . I will pay you later or whatever I have to do for you, I will do later. But you give me the channel today . . . that's just the way he operates.'

On 20 November 2009, Mehta's resignation was submitted to the Registrar of Companies in Mumbai. The letter reads, 'I, Kirit Chandulal Mehta, due to my personal reasons and other occupations, unable to continue as Chairman and Managing Director of M/S Aastha Broadcasting Network Limited.' That same day Shiv Kumar Garg, a minor shareholder in Ramdev's Vedic Broadcasting Ltd, was appointed to the post of chairman and executive additional director. Four months later Garg was elevated to the position of chairman and managing director.

~

There is no evidence on the public record to corroborate Mehta's version of events or confirm any wrongdoing on the part of Ramdev or his associates. While Mehta had initiated legal action against Ramdev in Mumbai shortly after he left for Dubai, he withdrew the case after his wife fell gravely ill and was diagnosed with cancer in 2012, partly hoping for an out-of-court settlement. Such a settlement never materialized.

Whether Mehta's version of events is true or not, what is clear is that Ramdev leaves in his wake a series of bad relationships and lingering questions. The bad blood between the Mehtas and him is not unique – it is just another example in a succession of partnerships that soured terribly.

Today, Vedic Broadcasting Ltd, that is, Baba Ramdev, is the sole owner of Aastha. S.K. Jain and Hiren Doshi continue to remain directors on its board and Pramod Joshi is its chief operations officer.

19

Mystery 3: The Mentor's Sudden Death

Haridwar, March 2010

Just months after taking over Aastha, the rival Sanskar channel came up for sale. 'Swamiji asked me to buy it, so I did,' says K.K. Pittie, one of Ramdev's biggest supporters. After he bought it Pittie ran the channel with Ramdev's advice, effectively putting Ramdev in charge of content on the two most important religious television channels in India.

Although Pittie had bought Sanskar channel at the behest of Ramdev, the issue of ownership began to strain relations between the two. Ramdev seemed to want to own the channel, not just call the shots. So Pittie handed it over to Swamiji as he valued their old relationship too much to ruin it over something like a channel.

In Ramdev's trademark barter style of operation, Pittie's young, dynamic son was given a range of distribution rights in return, something he feels very grateful for.

Meanwhile, by January 2010, the newly constructed Patanjali food park was opened. The park was expected to generate employment for 7000 people, and would be a runaway success.

As CMD of Patanjali Ayurveda overseeing the founding of the Patanjali Food and Herbal Park, Balkrishna had his hands full. He found his day-to-day management duties were keeping him away from Ramdev, the power fulcrum in Haridwar. Earlier, in October 2007, when Balkrishna was appointed managing director of Patanjali Ayurveda (though he was not entitled to draw a salary), it had intensified the rivalry between him and Ramdev's brother Ram Bharat, which was always bubbling beneath the surface. Now the two rivals would unite against a third ascendant force: Rajeev Dixit.

The man always standing beside Ramdev now was Rajeev Dixit, national secretary of the Bharat Swabhiman Andolan.

As mentioned earlier, Ramdev hoped to eventually convert the Bharat Swabhiman Andolan, technically a trust, into a full-fledged political party. With Ramdev's

Mystery 3: The Mentor's Sudden Death

ballooning political ambitions, Rajeev Dixit's importance also grew. He was now the key man, at the heart of all the action – adviser to and architect of Ramdev's socio-political messaging.

Balkrishna and Ram Bharat looked on resentfully as Rajeev Dixit, a suave outsider, far better educated and articulate than either of them, usurped their positions as advisers and became Ramdev's trusted political mentor. Such was the animosity between them that Dixit and Balkrishna would sometimes be in the same room and not acknowledge each other.

At the same time, Dixit's popularity was such that it was beginning to steal the limelight away from Ramdev himself. Yashdev Shastri, Ramdev's brother-in-law, was also jealous of Dixit, and had allegedly warned Ramdev not to give Dixit too much airtime: 'Or people will forget you and start following him.'

People familiar with the dynamic at the time say that Dixit's meteoric rise within Patanjali had begun to not only inspire internal jealousies and bitter rivalries but also help forge new alliances between old rivals Balkrishna and Ram Bharat. Facing the common threat of Dixit, they came together against him.

Roopesh Pandey, a former aide of Rajeev Dixit's, remembers getting a call from Ram Bharat sometime in 2009: 'He wanted to know more about Rajeev

Dixit's antecedents. He wanted to know how did a new guy like Rajeev Dixit become so close to Ramdev so quickly . . . he thought because I had left Rajeev Dixit's organization, I must have had a falling out with him and could be a source of damaging information,' says Pandey.

Dixit lived in a room not far from Ramdev's residence, and kept busy by travelling around the country on lecture tours. Even though he was estranged from his organization in Wardha, Dixit's old support base was far from lost to him. He had hundreds of thousands of followers across India.

About a year after founding the Bharat Swabhiman Trust, in March 2010, Ramdev kept his word and launched a political party. Under Dixit's guidance, the party made fighting corruption and black money the centrepiece of their message. When Ramdev unveiled his Bharat Swabhiman Party in New Delhi, he declared, 'I will field candidates from all the 543 constituencies of India and then there will be a revolution.'

Shortly after founding the party, in September 2010, in a bid to increase its membership, Ramdev and Dixit planned the Bharat Swabhiman yatra, where both leaders fanned out to various districts around the country to raise awareness for their movement and its goals.

But Dixit was not unaware that his presence in Haridwar and closeness to Ramdev was causing

Mystery 3: The Mentor's Sudden Death

unpleasantness. Madan Dubey, a long-time associate of Rajeev Dixit who continues to propound the views of the Azadi Bachao Andolan, says, 'He must have been troubled ... because that July [2010] when I asked him ... if I should also sign up to become a member of Bharat Swabhiman Andolan, he told me to wait. He told me he was not sure ... and that made me think there was something going on.'

~

Bemetara, November 2010

On 30 November 2010, two months after Ramdev and Rajeev Dixit began their nationwide Bharat Swabhiman yatra to drum up support for their party, Dixit was dead. He died on his forty-third birthday.

After a massive cardiac arrest, Dixit collapsed in a locked bathroom in an Arya Samaj guest house in the remote town of Bemetara in Chhattisgarh where he was delivering a lecture. Although he was rushed to a nearby hospital, he did not last through the night. According to Ramdev, Dixit had refused to have the medicines prescribed to him by the local doctor.

Pradeep Dixit says, 'The Bharat Swabhiman Andolan workers who were in Chhattisgarh with Rajeev called me when they were taking him to the hospital. I could not speak to him because they said he was not in a condition to talk ... By the time I reached him early the following morning, my brother was dead.'

But in a televised address on Aastha channel, Ramdev said that while he was not present with Dixit in Bemetara, he had spoken to him over the phone. Not just that, they had spoken for a whole hour about Dixit's poor health and line of treatment: *'Maine karib ek ghante tak unko samjhata raha, ek ghante tak! Bhai Rajeev, ab shareer mein dikkat aa rahi hai to ... unko shayad yeh genetic bimari thi ... BP ki, sugar ki, heart ki ... teeno.'* (I kept trying to explain to him for an hour, a whole hour! Brother Rajeev, there is a problem in your body ... He probably had a genetic condition of blood pressure, diabetes and heart disease ... all three.)

Pradeep Dixit cannot help but wonder now: how had his brother, who Ramdev's men had told him was in no condition to speak on the phone, managed to have an hour-long telephonic conversation with Ramdev about the ideal line of treatment? He also asserts that his brother suffered from no ailments and had never taken medicines for diabetes, blood pressure or a heart problem.

After Dixit died, a seemingly grief-stricken Ramdev had spoken to the family over the phone and requested them to allow him to arrange for the last rites on the

Mystery 3: The Mentor's Sudden Death

banks of the Ganga in order to honour him. The stunned family went along with Ramdev's plans. So, instead of taking Dixit's body back to Wardha where it would otherwise have been flown to, it was transported to Haridwar on a chartered plane.

By the next morning, hundreds of swadeshi activists from around the country were making their way to Haridwar to pay their respects to their leader. One of them was Madan Dubey. It had been nearly eighteen hours since Dixit's death when Dubey went to offer condolences to the family. Dixit's body lay in the Great Hall of Patanjali Yogpeeth II – an enormous space designed to allow thousands of people to do yoga together.

As an aside, Patanjali Yogpeeth II was an enormous campus with multiple auditoriums, nearly a thousand rooms to accommodate people, a free-of-charge hospice for a thousand people, a canteen, a museum, a food court to feed visitors, residential apartments for senior citizens, a sales outlet of 11,000 square feet, and the Bharat Swabhiman Trust office. Adjoining this campus lay another sprawling campus, Yog Gram, over 100 acres.

In the hall, mourners sat on mattresses and stood around in groups. Dixit's body lay on a block of ice, draped in white and orange. Marigold garlands and wreaths covered him. Only his face was visible, two balls of cotton stuffed into his nostrils.

But something was unsettling the onlookers: Dixit's face 'was unrecognizable ... a strange purple and blue. His skin was peeling strangely. There was some black, blue blood around his nose,' Dubey remembers. People huddled discussing Dixit's sudden death and the strange colour of his body. As more and more people streamed in, conspiracy theories about his death began to swirl wildly. Soon people began discussing the need for a postmortem.

Dubey finally said out loud what many were whispering: 'There has been foul play ... I want to know if anyone else feels that a postmortem should be conducted.'

He asked those who raised their hands to sign a petition addressed to Ramdev, demanding a postmortem before the cremation. By nightfall, there were fifty signatures on it.

At six the next morning, a group of nine men walked through grey winter mist to take the petition to Ramdev, only to be stopped by the guard who refused to let them enter the two-storey building complex where Ramdev used to live at that time. Dubey told the guard, 'All right then, please go and tell Babaji that if he does not meet us, Dixit's dead body will not be allowed to be cremated.'

Finally, Ramdev relented to a meeting at 7.30 a.m.,

Mystery 3: The Mentor's Sudden Death

and called in Dubey and his associates but 'only after taking away our cellphones, to make sure nothing was recorded,' Dubey recalls, a fear that even Kirit Mehta referred to during his fateful encounter with Ramdev.

Dubey sat closest to Ramdev – he had been appointed the speaker for his party. 'I gave him the petition, signed by fifty people, asking for a postmortem,' says Dubey. According to Dubey, this is how that meeting unfolded:

Ramdev asked, 'So what do you want?'

Dubey replied, 'All of us are trustees of the Azadi Bachao Andolan and we want a postmortem.'

'What is the need for it? This is a natural death.'

'We have our doubts. So, let's get a postmortem done. It's very simple.'

'But I spoke to the doctors myself. I have reports from the doctors that he had a heart attack and all that.'

'We don't trust it. We want a postmortem.'

'No, no ... I know it was a natural death.'

'How can you know? You were not there. You were only talking to them on the phone. How can you be sure there was no conspiracy?'

'But why will anyone conspire like that?'

'There can be many who might. You are well aware of it.'

Ramdev was growing angrier by the minute at what he must have seen as Dubey's insolence. He tried to rule out a postmortem saying it was against 'Hindu dharma'. But Dubey dismissed this objection saying, 'He [Rajeev Dixit] had no dharma. His dharma was the service of his country. He never called himself a man of any religion. So don't worry about Hindu dharma and get the postmortem done. It is good for you and it is good for us that all this becomes clear. Otherwise, fingers will be pointed ...'

But Ramdev was equally insistent. According to Dubey, he said, 'Such cutting and chopping is not done in Hindu dharma. A man is sent back the way he came.'

'It seems to me that you don't want the postmortem to be done.'

'Why would you say that?'

It was at this point that Dubey claims he became incredibly blunt: 'Rajeev Dixit did have fights with some of your people, didn't he? Your people had differences with him, didn't they? I know they were upset that some outsider like Rajeev Dixit came out of nowhere and became the national secretary of the Bharat Swabhiman Andolan. They were jealous that thousands of people used to come to meet him.'

This back and forth went on for over an hour, says Dubey. Finally, Ramdev suggested that they all go to the hall where Dixit's body lay, and ask the people there, and the Dixit family, for their opinion. This sounded like a reasonable thing to do.

Mystery 3: The Mentor's Sudden Death

But while Ramdev sat in his car with his people and sped off, Dubey and the others in his party followed on foot to the hall that was a twenty-minute walk away.

Before Dubey and Company could get there, a visibly angry Ramdev stormed into the hall, took the microphone and said, 'Some people have come from Mumbai. They want me to do a postmortem ... such cutting [of a dead body] is not permitted in Hindu dharma.'

One of the mourners present in the hall, a Dr Suman from Haryana who was closely involved with the work of the Bharat Swabhiman Andolan and Rajeev Dixit, stood up and said, 'So why aren't you getting it [a postmortem] done?' Ramdev was livid at being openly questioned, and was in no mood to answer.

Turning to his men, he commanded, 'Get the body ready for its final journey.' The cremation was originally scheduled for 11 a.m. It was still only nine.

Ramdev's men got the body ready for cremation, quickly carried it into an ambulance, and set off for the cremation ghats. 'We were just arriving at the hall after our walk from his house when we saw the ambulance driving away with Rajeevbhai's body in it,' remembers Dubey. 'We panicked and tried to stop the ambulance from leaving because we knew that once the body was cremated, our questions could never be answered,' says Dubey, his voice still filled with regret.

As the convoy drew up to the cremation ghats, where thousands of people had already gathered, Ramdev turned to Pradeep Dixit and suddenly said, 'Look, if you want, we can do the postmortem.'

Taken aback, Dixit said, 'Swamiji, all these people are already here. You have taken a decision for all of us not to do the postmortem. There is no point talking about it now, is there?'

When asked why he said this, Pradeep Dixit explains, 'What was I supposed to say? Everyone had reached the cremation ghat. I didn't know what to say ... People were whispering all kinds of things to me. If they were true then what was the guarantee that the postmortem report would not be doctored? ... I was not in a condition to defy him.'

~

The rumours that began that day have followed Ramdev ever since. On multiple occasions and at press conferences, he has addressed them head-on on Aastha, calling them an 'irresponsible, wicked conspiracy' against him.

Dubey, a lifelong friend and mentee of Rajeev Dixit's, says he will regret the moment of his cremation till his dying breath. 'After the cremation, when Rajeevbhai's laptop and his two phones were returned to his family,

Mystery 3: The Mentor's Sudden Death

they discovered that all three devices were completely wiped clean. All data on all three devices had been erased. I saw Rajeevji's room in Haridwar in a ransacked condition, things and documents missing from his room after his death ... I've felt absolutely sure that there was foul play in Rajeevbhai's death ... I know it. I saw the body. I will never stop saying it,' he asserts.

20

The Anna Movement

New Delhi, 2010–11

Rajeev Dixit may have gone but Ramdev's political ambitions were more alive than ever. There was no time to mourn his late adviser.

In mid November 2010, *Open* magazine published the Niira Radia tapes, recordings of a corporate lobbyist talking to some of India's top businessmen, journalists and politicians, in which she seemed to be lobbying for ministry allocations, and also engineering the sale of 2G spectrum. The spectrum sale, overseen by the UPA government, was believed to have caused a loss of Rs 1.76 trillion to the national exchequer.

But things had been nosediving for the government for a while before this. Since 2009 the list and scale of scandals it was embroiled in had been growing longer and more spectacular. Corruption was becoming a key electoral issue. By the end of 2010 the catalogue of scandals included the Satyam scam of Rs 14,000 crore, the Adarsh Housing Society scam where select government officials abused their power to subvert rules and regulations and grab prime government land for personal benefit, and the Commonwealth Games scam of Rs 70,000 crore.

Amid the widespread dissatisfaction among the people, a day after Rajeev Dixit's death, a budding anti-corruption movement spearheaded by seventy-three-year-old Anna Hazare, a celibate former truck driver in the Indian army; a former income tax officer, Arvind Kejriwal; a former police officer, Kiran Bedi; and Supreme Court lawyers Shanti and Prashant Bhushan, unveiled its version of the Lokpal bill: the Jan Lokpal bill. The government's draft of this bill to establish by law an anti-corruption watchdog or ombudsman was rumoured to be utterly toothless, while the Anna movement's bill gave the Lokpal sweeping powers. At that time the Lokpal was widely seen as a panacea for corruption, and the rage against the UPA's wheeling and dealing was channelled into the desire to build a strong Lokpal.

The kindling was ready, awaiting the match to be lit. And that match in those months of the Arab Spring

The Anna Movement

was Anna Hazare's movement that electrified people across India.

The leading lights of the movement were insisting that 'representatives from civil society' – this really meant just them – should be included on a drafting committee to overhaul the Lokpal bill that the government would then take to Parliament. In March 2011 Prime Minister Manmohan Singh even met Team Anna but didn't give in to their demand and the issue reached a stalemate.

Finally, on 5 April 2011, Hazare began a protest fast at Delhi's Jantar Mantar. The country watched the septuagenarian fight and struggle on their behalf, a tableau that many were touched by. As the hours of his fast ticked by, millions of Indians in 200 cities, from every class and religion, began to take to the streets. Defiant marches and vigils were held across the country in support of Hazare. The air was tense and volatile.

The anti-corruption plank of Ramdev's Bharat Swabhiman Andolan had already drawn him close to Team Anna. But it was now that Ramdev made a flamboyant entry into the campaign and on to the centre stage of a national political drama.

Two days after the fast began, the quiet, drained Anna Hazare, was eclipsed by the colourful, orange-robed Ramdev who had a knack for drawing and mesmerizing an audience. Striding and swishing on the stage, Ramdev exhorted supporters with cries of *'Anna aage badho, hum tumhare saath hain.'* (Anna, charge ahead, we are with you.)

He laid moral claim to sharing the stage with Anna Hazare by joining him in fasting. Ramdev announced: 'Anna is not the only man fasting today. I have fasted with him since the first day and I'm fasting today too.' Then, pulling his orange shawl aside, he bared his torso and sucked in his stomach until it was a pit framed by his ribs. He told a wild audience, 'Look, you can check it if you like!' The crowds cheered and even those on the stage smiled. Ramdev laughed with the crowds.

In the face of mounting public pressure, the government blinked. On 9 April it issued a gazette notification agreeing to a joint committee of civil society and government representatives for drafting a more effective Lokpal bill. Anna Hazare – and Ramdev – could break their fasts.

Ramdev had flawlessly managed to inveigle himself on to a national stage and establish himself as an integral leader of India's anti-corruption movement. He smoothly abandoned his old allies in the Congress who had helped him build Patanjali. Yet another alliance, with a powerful national political party, which had helped Ramdev become a major national player, was soon to come to a bitter end.

~

Ramlila grounds, 4 June 2011

The first meeting to draft the new Lokpal bill took place in North Block, which houses the ministries of finance and home, on 16 April 2011, a week after Anna Hazare had broken his fast. Hazare, Arvind Kejriwal, Prashant Bhushan, Shanti Bhushan and Justice Santosh Hegde were now members of the joint committee for drafting the Lokpal bill. Peace had, at least temporarily, been restored.

But while the country waited for the government to draft a new legislation, Ramdev added his own demands to the ones made by Team Anna – that the government nationalize black money unlawfully sent abroad by Indians and also declare such transfers prosecutable as treason.

Given Ramdev's popularity, the government couldn't ignore his demand for the return of black money to India. They had to respond, even if only to discredit Ramdev. His former allies in the powerful Congress party now accused him of land grabbing, corruption and money laundering through donations received by his trusts. In May 2011 Digvijay Singh called him a 'thug' and a 'money-launderer'. He belittled – and underestimated – Ramdev by saying, 'Many people turned up to persuade Anna Hazare to give up his fast. It is possible that no one might come to the aid of Ramdev. It will be better if he does not observe the fast.'

Ramdev, of course, launched a vigorous defence: in a televised interview on Aaj Tak, he energetically dismissed the allegations as baseless. Such accusations were not unusual for a person such as himself, he asserted. 'Take Bhagwan Ram, Bhagwan Krishna, Prophet Mohammed, Adi Shankracharya or Swami Dayanand Maharshi...now I sit in front of you. History shows everyone who led movements against injustice has faced charges. I can respond if the allegations have some basis. What do I say to baseless allegations?' he asked the audience. Ramdev wasn't about to back down and held increasingly aggressive press conferences.

Though Ramdev shared the stage with Anna Hazare, his movement was seen as distinct from Hazare's, which was all about the Lokpal bill. Ramdev, on the other hand, was making more radical demands on black money. To bolster his movement, he made overtures to some members of Anna's former team, including Justice Santosh Hegde, who refused to join his movement.

But Ramdev soldiered on, and served the government

an ultimatum. He would begin an indefinite fast in Delhi on 4 June 2011 until the government acceded to his demands on black money. Ramdev was anxious that his fast also draw as large crowds and be as visible and popular as Anna's had been.

While Congress spokesperson Digvijay Singh attacked Ramdev in public, the party was rattled enough to send envoys to him in private. 'I used to go all the time to talk to Ramdev to see if we could find a peaceful solution to all this,' remembers Subodh Kant Sahay, then minister for food processing industries, under whose watch Ramdev had acquired permissions for his food park. 'But there was a growing belief within the party that Ramdev was not acting on his own. There was a belief that politics was driving his agitation.'

Ramdev was aware of these suspicions, and even told K.N. Govindacharya not to meet him while the agitation progressed 'because he did not want to send the wrong signal [that he was in cahoots with the RSS and BJP] to the Congress party'. Govindacharya agreed to this, 'because even though we were not a part of his agitation, we certainly wanted him to succeed ... as did the rest of the country'.

On 1 June, as pressure on the government built up, a chartered plane took off from Ujjain in Madhya Pradesh with Ramdev on board. Around noon, major news networks covered its landing in Delhi because, in an unprecedented gesture, four senior cabinet ministers, Pranab Mukherjee, P.K. Bansal, Kapil Sibal and Subodh Kant Sahay, were waiting at the airport to welcome Ramdev – so terrified was the government of Ramdev's hunger strike. This was Ramdev's shining moment, a moment that affirmed how powerful he had become – a high-profile contingent of the Union cabinet had been dispatched to plead with him to call off his agitation. They talked for two hours and agreed to meet again the next day.

From this point on the story becomes hazy. Each player asserts a different version of the truth.

Despite hectic back-channel negotiations in the following days, Ramdev declared his intentions of going ahead with his fast on 4 June.

Platoons of his followers began arriving at Ramlila grounds in the national capital in anticipation of the fast-unto-death. On D-day, after a series of long, rambling speeches, towards evening, Ramdev announced to the tentful of about 40,000 followers that the government had acceded to his demands, but he did not call off his fast.

Apparently, an informal agreement – expressed in a handwritten and signed letter by Balkrishna – had been reached between the two parties at the Claridges hotel in Lutyens' Delhi the previous day. This was to be translated into a formal, binding agreement in order for the fast to be called off. But this formal agreement was never finalized – even after Ramdev agreed in private to call off his fast. It was almost as though neither party trusted the other to keep its word. The situation deteriorated into a bitter exchange of accusations and counter-accusations between the government and Ramdev. A furious Ramdev accused the government of betrayal and foul play. And the government, fed up with having to grovel to Ramdev, charged him with backtracking and having a political motivation that went beyond his purported fight against corruption and black money.

Within hours of this war of words, the police began gathering at the venue of Ramdev's protest. An hour after midnight, they swooped down on the sleeping protesters, forcibly evicting them with tear gas and a lathi-charge. In the ensuing chaos Ramdev, believing his life was in danger, leapt off the stage and melted into the crowds below. Borrowing the clothes of a close female aide, he drew under the stage and hurriedly disguised himself as a woman – bushy beard notwithstanding. Then, dressed in a white salwar kameez and with a dupatta covering his face, he tried to escape from the protest venue. Unsuccessfully.

Ramdev was arrested while trying to escape posing as an injured woman, his arms draped over his companions' shoulders. The police gave him a fresh set of orange clothes and put him on a plane back to Dehradun with the instructions that he should not re-enter Delhi for fifteen days.

But when Ramdev got off the plane to waiting cameras in Haridwar, he was still wearing the white salwar kameez. During interviews he repeatedly stood up to show reporters the indignity he had been reduced to in order to escape the UPA's brutal crackdown. In the days to come he would even accuse the government of trying to kill him.

Ramdev seemed to have been truly rattled. He had lost his sharp political instinct and couldn't see how silly he looked. He had instantly gone from national anti-corruption warrior to laughing stock.

The agitation had failed and he had made a formidable enemy. The Congress would likely never ally with him again. This must have been a new feeling for Ramdev since he was used to always being friends with those in power. It must have been terrifying to think that the state was going to come after him.

He had made his play and it had gone horribly wrong.

21

The Old Mentor Re-enters

Noida, October 2011

Although Karamveer had a yoga camp going on in Noida, he delayed his arrival in Delhi by a day. He dearly wished to avoid being in the city on a day Ramdev was also scheduled to be there for his own yoga camp. 'I thought if I delayed my arrival in the city, I would manage to avoid him [Ramdev] entirely,' Karamveer recalls.

A few months after Ramdev tried to evade arrest by cross-dressing, television stations were still running humiliating footage of him in women's clothes every time his name came up.

Karamveer, his former mentor, friend and adviser, felt oddly pleased. But in the face of a government keen on revenge, Ramdev was reaching out again, desperate to meet. Karamveer's phone kept ringing. Ramdev was calling incessantly. But Karamveer was equally desperate to avoid meeting Ramdev. For him, their parting in 2005 had been final.

~

The government had trained its guns on Patanjali and seemed to be running a smear campaign against Ramdev and his associates. On 20 July 2011 Acharya Balkrishna was arrested – and shortly after let go – by the CBI for allegedly using forged documents to acquire an Indian passport. The CBI claimed that his 'Purva Madhyama' (high school degree) and Shastri (a Sanskrit degree) from Sampurna Nand Sanskrit University were fake.

On 24 July the CBI registered a case against him under sections 420 (cheating), 468 and 471 (forgery) and 120-B (criminal conspiracy) of the Indian Penal Code and for violating section 12 of the Passport Act (knowingly furnishing false documents to get a passport). The very next morning, Balkrishna disappeared from the Kankhal ashram, and resurfaced only after the Uttarakhand High Court granted him a stay on arrest. But Balkrishna could not evade arrest forever: in July 2012 he had to spend a month in jail before the courts granted him bail. The case is still ongoing in the Uttarakhand High Court. Ramdev, with his trademark energy, cried foul and accused

The Old Mentor Re-enters

the government of manufacturing cases against them. But this did not stop notices from flying at them, thick and fast – from the Allahabad High Court issuing a notice to Ramdev in July 2011 to respond to charges of making derogatory remarks about Buddhism to a September 2011 investigation by the Enforcement Directorate against Ramdev for Forex Exchange Management Act (FEMA) violations. In September 2011 the government also issued a notice to Ramdev asking for information about the foreigners living in his ashram, alleging that he was sheltering unreported Bangladeshi nationals. The government also issued a tax evasion notice to one of Ramdev's trusts, demanding Rs 5 crore payable as tax on fees collected from those learning yoga.

Allegations of FEMA violations, land grabbing, money laundering all swirled in the media too. It was impossible to sort truth from falsehood and even ardent followers began wondering about the bona fides of Baba Ramdev.

One of the allegations, made by Congress minister Digvijay Singh, was that Ramdev was a 'thug' and that 'they' (Ramdev and Balkrishna) had stolen from Shankar Dev and Karamveer, both founding members of their first trust, Divya Yog Mandir. Shankar Dev had disappeared in a trailing cloud of mystery, but Karamveer was still around. Ramdev must have thought that he could be used to fight this new onslaught.

His back against the wall, Ramdev understandably felt it necessary to combat these allegations by a show of friendship and solidarity with Karamveer. He must also have realized that if he could demonstrate that one of the government's many allegations against him was false – and therefore motivated – then he could convince people that the rest were untrue too.

To this end, he now needed his old friend Karamveer more than ever before. But Karamveer had left in a huff seven years ago, never to return. If only Ramdev could convince Karamveer to share the stage with him doing yoga for a few minutes, say they were still friends, he would have a fighting chance. Therefore, the incessant calls to Karamveer.

Karamveer's plan of avoiding Ramdev in Delhi did not work. Ramdev coaxed and cajoled Karamveer by citing the enormous trouble he was in until Karamveer finally agreed to attend his yoga camp. Perhaps Karamveer agreed for old times' sake and for the affection he may still have had for his protégés, perhaps he was just too kind not to help someone in distress, or perhaps he too felt the government was witch-hunting Ramdev.

Next, Ramdev began to work on Karamveer to sit on the stage with him and to stay the night at the camp. Karamveer flatly refused. But Ramdev wasn't one to listen. In the dead of night there was a huge commotion

The Old Mentor Re-enters

at the gate to Karamveer's own yoga camp. Ramdev and his people had come to fetch him!

'We were so surprised to see that Baba Ramdev and some of his people had come to us,' remembers Vipin Pradhan, Karamveer's nephew. Pradhan continues to live in the Haridwar area and helps his uncle with yoga camps whenever he can.

'My uncle was . . . concerned for Ramdev's safety,' Pradhan recalls. 'But I knew why Baba Ramdev had come – he was there in our camp only to ensure that my uncle kept his word and went to his programme the next day.'

'That was how and why I was on his stage that day,' says Karamveer. During his televised talk at the camp, Ramdev addressed thousands of attendees and called it a historic day, 'because for the first time after 2005, Shraddheya Shri Karamveerji Maharaj has joined us again on stage. Please welcome him, so that he feels the welcome is not from hundreds, thousands or lakhs, but he feels the welcome of crores of Indians who have joined our cause. We were together then, we are together now and we will be together until our last dying breath.'

With that Digvijay Singh's allegations – regarding Karamveer at least – seemed to have been successfully neutralized.

~

A few months later, Karamveer got another burst of calls from Ramdev and Balkrishna. Ramdev's desperation to defend himself was mounting as the government refused to abandon its pursuit of him and his empire. Ramdev's movement against corruption had also by then devolved into a one-point agenda – *Congress hatao, desh bachao* (Remove the Congress from power to save the country).

Again Karamveer relented, and agreed to be seen with them in Delhi. Things seemed to have come full circle. At the beginning of their association, Ramdev and Balkrishna needed Karamveer to give them the legitimacy of his learning and character. In 2011, again, they needed Karamveer's goodness to reflect well on them.

22

The CEO

Haridwar, 2011–14

S.K. Patra, a jovial, balding man with discoloured teeth, remembers a sudden summons from Ramdev when he was CEO of Bhanu Farms, a food processing venture in Jabalpur owned by the Kolkata-based Bangur conglomerate, one of Asia's richest, with expertise in commodities such as cement and jute, and, of course, food processing. 'Ramdev had gotten to know about my antecedents and was very keen that I come and join them,' says Patra, slightly self-important though an undeniably credible witness..

In the five years since the formation of Patanjali Ayurveda Limited in January 2006, the company had undergone a metamorphosis. Patanjali had moved from being a yoga-events-based company and Ayurvedic pharmacy to debuting in food processing. Its units processed juice from amla, apple and aloe vera, as well as processed corn, soyabean, barley, oats and millets, and produced packaged spices and soaps. Patanjali Ayurveda was growing stunningly: On 31 March 2011, the last day of the financial year 2010–11, the company reported its first doubling of revenues from Rs 167 crore to Rs 317 crore.

But the company was about to hit a roadblock. Balkrishna, under Ramdev's direction, had tried to put in place the nuts and bolts for the Patanjali food park. But in April 2011 a host of top employees managing the food park suddenly – and mysteriously – quit the company. This included the IIM-educated CEO of the food park, C.L. Kamal, who had been with Patanjali since 2009.

With the core leadership team gone, the nascent Patanjali food park understandably began to flounder. Patanjali Ayurveda also had to indefinitely halt its ambitious plans to expand into activities related to the manufacture of dyes and paints, clothing, and power generation and distribution. It was then that a desperate Ramdev called Patra.

Patra's credentials were unimpeachable. An IIT-trained engineer, he had had a long and successful career spanning four decades in post-harvest technologies and food processing. While Patra was reluctant to meet Ramdev and take his offer any further, his wife, impressed with Ramdev's work in the ongoing anti-corruption movement, insisted that Patra should at least meet him. But once he reached Haridwar, one thing led to another and Patra never looked back: he was seduced and coaxed by Ramdev into joining him, a decision Patra came to regret deeply. It seems hard for people to refuse Ramdev.

As Patra wandered the halls of Patanjali Yogpeeth that April, took in the scale of Yog Gram, watched the nation's leaders quaking in fear of Ramdev, it must have been tempting to ally with him. Little did Patra know that things were about to change dramatically.

~

Within days of the midnight police swoop at his protest site in June, Ramdev was, as mentioned earlier, clobbered by political controversies and notices from various government agencies including the Reserve Bank of India and the Enforcement Directorate. On 7 June 2011 *India Today* reported that the CBI and the income tax department had launched probes into Ramdev's thirty-four companies.

The CBI enquiry into Balkrishna's passport followed four weeks later and is still ongoing, as is the Enforcement Directorate's investigation into FEMA violations and charges of money laundering. If the FEMA violations are proved, they would only carry a financial penalty, but if the charges regarding Balkrishna's passport are upheld by the court, he may be imprisoned for two years.

Ramdev's fallout with the government also resulted in the reopening of investigations into the disappearance of Shankar Dev by the CBI. Ramdev appeared on a Times Now show in conversation with Arnab Goswami and said that the reinvestigation was a part of the Congress conspiracy against him using its 'dirty tricks department'. He alleged that the government was conspiring to fabricate evidence against him to implicate him in murder and a 'drugs, sex and tax racket'.

The debacle at the Ramlila grounds had derailed the momentum that Ramdev's Bharat Swabhiman Party had gathered. It seemed that Ramdev's political career was finished. For anyone else this may have been a reasonable conclusion to draw. But Ramdev has a remarkable ability to fight back. The boy from Said Alipur had not come this far by being a quitter. He'd taken on the government and very nearly brought it down. With his television channels, he could easily do this again. When he told millions of people across the country that the government was unfairly persecuting him, most believed him. Undeniably, the government's relentless pursuit did have the whiff of vindictive persecution.

The CEO

Ramdev became the rallying call of a resistance movement. It brought him new allies who were powerful, politically savvy and waiting in the wings to seize power in New Delhi.

But while Ramdev was scheming and strategizing, and Balkrishna was fighting serious charges of forgery, neither had the mental bandwidth for business.

~

When Ramdev bullied Patra into joining Patanjali Ayurveda Limited and help run the new food park, Ramdev's empire consisted of four trusts (with a declared turnover of Rs 1100 crore), thirty-four companies whose fortunes were largely tied to each other through a complex web of financial dealings, and large landholdings in various people's names. It is difficult to put a precise value to this nest of companies, with its shared group of directors and shareholders and co-dependent revenue streams, but a good guestimate would be somewhere in the ballpark of Rs 250 crore in 2010–11. Ramdev was ridiculously lucky to have Patra, a complete outsider, at the helm of his empire.

Patanjali Ayurveda Limited and the food park were in a dire situation indeed, says Patra. With CBI and income tax notices flying thick and fast, the task of establishing a food park must have seemed daunting to Patra. The government has enormous powers to harass the unfriendly, and so Patanjali would see the environment ministry send it a notice for pollution one day, and a boiler man show up and threaten to shut down the factory the next.

Ramdev and Balkrishna defended themselves by repeatedly pointing out that hundreds of Patanjali's employees would be out of jobs if they were out of business. But the government seemed to be on a mission to destroy them.

Within weeks of joining Ramdev's empire, Patra realized he was Patanjali's chief firefighter. Recalling his early days there, Patra says, 'I found myself holding their Patanjali baby.' Two weeks after the Ramlila fiasco, the government threatened to withdraw its approval for Ramdev's food park, saying that the park's activities had to remain separate from those of Patanjali Ayurveda Limited. Patra had to go on a charm offensive, and somehow convince government officials that the food park was, in fact, *their* baby. Patra, who had long years of experience working with the government, convinced the bureaucrats that he was their man in Patanjali and knew how to clean up the mess the food park was in and get it off the ground.

But the government was not the only stumbling block; Ramdev's enterprise was facing some fundamental challenges. While Ramdev certainly has a shrewd business sense, his expansion till then had been haphazard and lacked a cohesive strategic vision.

'He went for many plants. Because he was flush with funds and he was itching for investments ... A chawanprash plant, one flour factory came up almost instantly. He began importing really good machines from all around the world – extraction units, colour extractions and packaging for bottles, cartons. He manufactured his own packaging,' Patra says, admiring of Ramdev's vigour but critical of his overextension of Patanjali. Most of the new machinery had not even been unpacked. A brand-new juice plant was lying unused, there were cold storage issues, and huge inefficiencies in the usage of food processing units – for instance, a flour mill with a capacity of producing 100 metric tonnes of flour a day was producing only two metric tonnes a day. The reason for this investment spree, according to Patra, is that Ramdev was looking for an outlet for all the 'disorganized funds' he was getting through his yoga programmes and donations.

The company was plagued by a lack of professionalism. Patanjali products were yet to undergo tests and get quality control approvals, and most of their employees were untrained. A culture of debating product feasibility, market research and competition analysis was lacking. Rather than first deciding what they wanted to produce and then building the infrastructure to support it,

Ramdev was used to first pumping in raw financial power to build generic FMCG-related plants and purchasing machinery and only then asking what they really wanted to make with it.

Patra remembers Ramdev's overwhelming urge to produce and market absolutely everything that a person consumes or uses throughout the day. 'Toothbrush, toothpaste, juices, daliya, salt, soap, detergents, cosmetics ... Baba wanted to make it all.'

So Patra's first order of business was fairly clear: clean up the mess. To begin with, he needed to disentangle one company from another. Not only did several of Ramdev's companies share the same manufacturing and office space – this was the government's objection regarding the Patanjali food park, technically a separate company – but they also gave contracts to each other and had a tangled web of ownership.

Patra engaged hordes of chartered accountants whose sole job was to segregate the companies. He also physically separated the food park from the other Patanjali companies to address the government's concerns.

By August 2011 Balkrishna had struck a tentative truce with the government. He returned to focus on Divya Pharmacy and the manufacture of Ayurvedic drugs – these were activities that didn't come under the Patanjali Ayurveda Limited or Patanjali food park umbrella, Patra's domain. The pharmacy was thriving. Ramdev, in the meantime, was focusing on Aastha and yoga, and, of course, his anti-Congress and pro-BJP political agenda. While Ramdev's brother Ram Bharat was involved with Patanjali Ayurveda, Patra had a free hand in the day-to-day functioning. He had to run only major business decisions past Ramdev. According to Patra, Ramdev took a huge personal interest in his products. He would try out his new products personally and give feedback. 'Baba has ... robust common sense, business sense that I must admire,' says Patra.

But Ramdev was also given to hyperbole, which irritated Patra. 'He did not know his own numbers. He'd throw whatever number came into his head. With a 100 crores turnover, he used to say "*Main Hindustan Lever ko bhaga doonga, ITC ko bhaga doonga.* [I'll make Hindustan Lever and ITC run away.]" He used to keep talking like that, big fiery speeches against multinational companies,' Patra sighs. But when Patra said it was fine to demonize the multinationals but it was their procedures and professionalism that Patanjali had to adopt, Ramdev was astute enough to realize the value of that advice. That, Patra said, was the only way to succeed. Soon an overhaul of Patanjali was under way.

Patra invited experts from multinational companies and gave them targets to build standard operating procedures (SOP) for each machine in each plant. The

SOP guidelines directed plant managers about the smallest of details – from how to check raw material quality to how to feed it into the machine, at what time, at what temperature, etc. Constrained by an ill-trained workforce, Patra was trying to build a framework so that the quality of the end product was assured. Products were standardized according to quality norms laid down by the government.

It took about a year, but in the end the SOPs were printed – 'Big, big books, like bibles,' recalls Suresh Kanthaliya, who worked closely with Patra during those days. Simultaneously, Patra had been busy hiring highly trained technocrat-managers, new factory workers who were intensively briefed before they were sent out to work on the factory floor.

But SOPs are no magic bullet and Patra had to constantly rally his troops to follow the procedures that had been so painstakingly laid out.

After much hard toil, the nuts and bolts seemed to be in place.

~

According to Patra, his success and Ramdev's increasing reliance on him were, as usual, sparking jealousies in Ramdev's innermost circle: Balkrishna and Ram Bharat. And despite Patra's efforts at professionalizing the enterprise and following industry best practices, cronyism was still rampant at Patanjali Ayurveda Limited. People up and down the organization were drawn from Ramdev's family networks. Ramdev's 'kitchen cabinet' of sycophants created daily confusion and had neither vision nor skill to see the organization as a whole.

'It was chaos every day. Production guys saying the ingredients are not there, sales guy yelling that inventory was not in place, quality control guy then stops production somewhere ... it just could not work like that!' says Patra, looking exasperated even after all these years.

During his tenure with K.K. Birla's Chambal Fertilizers and Chemicals Ltd, Patra had learnt to make a daily summary of the organization through a unique network of cross-functional committees. Drawing from that idea, Patra set up thirty committees covering every aspect of the business from purchasing and production to market research and canteen management, and created a schedule for their mandatory meetings. At the end of each meeting, minutes would be laid before Patra, and if there were any disputes, they would be settled by him. 'My job became very simple then,' Patra explains, satisfied that he had ironed out the kinks in the day-to-day functioning of such a huge conglomerate. 'It is not possible to scale something as vast ... without the skeleton, the bones in place to allow it to function seamlessly.'

The production side taken care of, Patra's next task was to attend to marketing and sales. Up till then, Ramdev used to advertise his products for free on Aastha. And the sales outlets were mostly run by people known to him, including some relatives.

Patra was determined to change this. An FMCG giant cannot be built without a solid distribution and retail network, or without advertising budgets. Patra told Ramdev that if he wanted to go from revenues of Rs 250 crore a year to Rs 1000 crore, he would have to shell out some money for marketing and advertising. Ramdev agreed to grant Patra a marketing budget of Rs 20 crore. This was still a measly sum and Ramdev only really started advertising properly much later, around 2015.

But having somewhat understood the significance of advertising, Ramdev also used his connections and his earthy business style to clinch deals. He bartered, for instance, excess chawanprash inventory worth Rs 2 crore to a well-connected newspaper proprietor in return for Rs 4 crore of advertising in his papers, Patra recalls with grudging admiration. (The newspaper proprietor apparently planned to distribute the chawanprash to thousands of his employees across the country.)

Armed with his marketing budget, Patra set about hiring a sales force of 200 people post-haste.

The CEO

Part of the secret of Patanjali's success is its threefold distribution network that Patra helped build. Patra analysed the distribution contracts of the large FMCG multinationals and finally created Patanjali's own model. They decided to have super distributors, who would oversee five or six distributors who would in turn each manage fifteen to twenty retailers. The advantage of a super distributor was that, unlike the model others followed, he bought the goods outright and they were no longer Patanjali's responsibility. This distributor–super distributor network was built in addition to an existing network of 5000-odd seva and arogya kendras that functioned as Ayurvedic doctors' clinics, pharmacies and retails points for Patanjali Ayurveda products.

But in his efforts to streamline Patanjali Ayurveda's distribution Patra again came up against entrenched interests. Until then, distribution was limited to people close to Ramdev. When Patra opened it up, the entrenched insiders opposed the move. 'There was internal political pressure on the Baba. So I met with the Baba and told him: "Baba, take none of their recommendations. Make me your villain. Tell them, 'I don't know anything. He's just done it.' Otherwise this is not going to work. Every other person will have some agenda and try to influence you ... just blame me,"' Patra recalls suggesting to Ramdev.

'There is a critical time in the life of every organization

that determines if what you have built is going to take off or not. This was that time for Patanjali,' says Patra. It was also going to determine if he could make good on his promise to Ramdev and drive up turnover by nearly five times to Rs 1000 crore.

Patra appointed some of his top people to liaise with the new super distributors to help them find their bearings. Then began the appointment of distributors under the super distributors. For the first three months, they had no sales targets at all. All Patra asked his employees was: 'How many super distributors did you make? How many distributors? How many retailers?' He says, 'That was their performance yardstick...those months I did not care at all if inventory was moving or not. A network had to be built up first.'

Patra's efforts began to pay off almost immediately: Patanjali Ayurveda's turnover increased to Rs 446 crore in 2012, from Rs 317 crore at the end of 2010–11. Ramdev realized that they could realistically touch the Rs 1000 crore mark soon and that was their next target.

The ensuing plan to power such growth required another distribution channel, apart from the arogya and seva kendras, and super distributor network – a network of freelance retailers. A new network of one lakh 'swadeshi kendras' was to be established. These swadeshi kendras were pre-existing stores that would lease part of their shop floor space for Patanjali products.

The CEO

In return they would be allowed to use Ramdev's image for their store branding. Ordinarily, an existing network of distributors and super distributors would have protested such an infringement on their rights, but Patanjali Ayurveda cleverly offered them a 1 per cent commission on all sales made by the freelancers. The idea was a hit. After all, 'It was money without work for them, so they agreed,' says Patra smiling.

However, translating such an ambitious idea into reality was not easy. That is when the Bharat Swabhiman Andolan's membership was sought to be harnessed. With Ramdev's political future in question, the organization had been at a loose end.

One thousand of their members were given a salary of Rs 5000 a month and sent off to help Patanjali Ayurveda establish a network of freelance distributors. The idea of 'serving the country by promoting swadeshi, a.k.a. Patanjali products' fired the Bharat Swabhiman sevaks.

Gunendar Kapur, a leading retail and consumer executive who had worked for over a decade at Unilever before joining as CEO and president of Reliance Retail, commended the structure: 'His distribution is very different. He has these dedicated distributors and franchisee stores. He puts an Ayurveda doctor in the shop, who prescribes things also available there.'

With these measures in place, distribution simply

exploded. Pictures of Ramdev loomed over cities, towns and villages. Ayurveda was also catching up in popularity. It had never before been propagated in such an organized fashion. Ramdev was now associated with everything healthy, everything 'Indian' and, automatically, everything he sold was seen as wholesome, pure and good. It was no surprise then that in some places even stores that were not officially carrying Patanjali products put up his pictures over their shopfronts.

Production could barely keep up and battalions of trucks left Patanjali factories loaded with products night and day. Realizing he'd begun paying truckers a small fortune, Ramdev set up his own logistics company. So now even most of the trucks ferrying his products belonged to him.

'Everything became perfectly streamlined and formalized – stocking, processing, production – to match demand to supply,' remembers Patra, still delighted with how it had all worked out perfectly, like clockwork.

~

By the time 2013 rolled around, Patanjali Ayurveda factories were churning out 500 products, and hundreds of new products were being tested. Thirty scientists at Patanjali laboratories were innovating food products, Ayurvedic medicines and cosmetics every day. A steady stream of products went into Ramdev's office for his personal inspection and approval.

Then, according to Patra, came a big bang – honey. 'We simply bought honey from many different suppliers, refined it, processed it, packaged it, put our label and sold it. As Patanjali honey was the cheapest it quickly swept up the market,' says Patra, explaining that it was the success of honey that made him think of ghee – a product that was destined to catapult Patanjali into the big league.

When he found a ghee producer (who worked earlier for a competing brand, Gowardhan), Patra hired his plant at first. It took him only days to realize the demand was explosive. 'We needed to expand production within days! We started sourcing white butter ... in truckloads ... A few hundred tonnes was produced at first. Now, every day, Ramdev is manufacturing 100 tonnes of ghee. Can you imagine? And every ghee bottle is giving him a profit of fifty to sixty rupees. Each one,' says Patra.

Startlingly, according to Patra, what Patanjali often sells as 'cow' ghee is not cow ghee at all. It is actually ghee that is made from white butter that is, in turn, made of the milk of various animals, not just cows, that is procured from small and marginal producers in various parts of the country, including Maharashtra and Karnataka. (White butter precedes ghee in the production process and is not as nutritious. While white butter contains butterfat and milk solids, ghee contains only butterfat. If white butter is cooked until all the milk solids are caramelized and strained, you get ghee. Ghee, now proven to be lactose- and casein-free, is not only a stable, nutrient-rich fat, but also a source of good cholesterol.)

Nandini, for instance, a milk brand owned by the Karnataka Co-operative Milk Producer's Federation, is reportedly one of the largest suppliers of white butter to Ramdev. It collects milk from 23 lakh milk producers in 22,000 villages of the state and does not separate milk based on its source (as cow milk, buffalo milk or goat milk).

So the white butter that reaches Ramdev's factories is derived from the milk of not just cows but buffaloes and goats too. All that Ramdev does to it is melt the sourced white butter, strain it and add some herbs to it to convert it into ghee. Ramdev 'claims this is all cow's ghee ... but who knows? Is it cow ghee or buffalo ghee or goat ghee ... even Ramdev does not know! He cannot know! But there it is ... 1500 crore of his business,' remarks Patra.

Ramdev goes one step further. He sells his ghee as desi cow ghee. The distinction of the source of milk is important and has far-reaching ramifications on health. According to Keith Woodford, professor of farm management and agribusiness at Lincoln University in

New Zealand and author of *Devil in the Milk: Illness, Health and Politics of A1 and A2 Milk*, there is a clear link between the milk we drink and a range of serious illnesses such as diabetes, heart disease, autism and schizophrenia. Woodford asserts that mixed breed cows, such as jersey cows, contain the A1 beta-casein which triggers an adverse reaction in the human body when digested. On the other hand, the milk of many herds of Asia (including local Indian pure breed cows such as the *Bos indicus*) contain A2 protein – which is safer for human consumption.

Yet when Ramdev sells a kilo of what he calls 'Desi Cow Ghee', not only can he not be sure that it is 'desi' – he cannot even be sure that it is cow ghee.

As mentioned earlier, Ramdev's vision for Patanjali is that he wants to produce everything that an ordinary Indian needs from sunrise to sunset. Patanjali Ayurveda even produces salt. Salt is a 10,000-crore-rupee organized industry in India. Under Patra, Patanjali Ayurveda tied up with a salt producer in Gujarat. Ramdev began to buy in bulk from them, iodize and pack the salt, and sell it. Today while a one-kilo packet of Tata salt costs Rs 20, Aashirwad Rs 18 and Saffola Rs 31, Patanjali sells it for Rs 12.

So what's their secret? According to Patra, 'Baba never cared about what the market prices were. For any product pricing, he was personally involved. He would ask how much it had cost to produce something. Then with a slim margin – he just wanted to sell.' Gunendar Kapur agrees, 'He doesn't seem to care much about the money, he cares about his own legacy. His margins are very, very low. For formal companies a profit after tax of less than 15 per cent is too low. Their investors will not be happy with that kind of a performance ... Ramdev does not have such a limitation.'

But it is not as though Ramdev does not care about profits at all. Some of his products have premium prices: ghee and toothpaste, for instance. One litre of Patanjali ghee is nearly 25 per cent more expensive than one litre of ghee from leading rival brands such as Amul or Gits. Similarly, now priced at Rs 75, Patanjali's Dant Kanti toothpaste is about 42 per cent more expensive than Colgate Cibaca's Vedshakti.

~

Patra had taken the business to great heights. But by the end of 2013, little over two years after taking over as CEO of Patanjali Ayurveda and the Patanjali food park, the trouble and friction started. Until then Ramdev was focusing largely on an alliance with the BJP, and making sure that the party won the 2014 general elections. He was also able to spend more time on his companies and the free rein that Patra had been given began to be tightened.

This was not a pleasant experience for Patra. Earlier, whenever Ramdev arrived at the company, Patra would be expected to touch Ramdev's feet and sit on the floor under him, just like all the other employees. This had always troubled him a little, because it meant his subordinates viewed him as a 'guru-bhai' (disciple-brother of the same guru), rather than as their boss. Yet, Patra had tolerated it because Ramdev was hardly ever around. But now, he found himself more and more often at Ramdev's feet.

But it was not just the compulsory obsequiousness that Patra found disconcerting. Ramdev and he had fundamental disagreements over money. Though Patra was doing two jobs – he was CEO of Patanjali Ayurveda and was also overseeing the food park – Ramdev was paying him for only one role, according to Patra.

Even that was after a hard-fought battle, and Ramdev, says Patra, was itching to stop that salary payment too. Ramdev termed, and viewed, the labour of his employees as 'seva', or service. The idea of renaming work as seva was an organization-wide phenomenon at Patanjali Ayurveda, says Patra. This renaming may seem trivial to an outsider, but it cleverly does two things: first, it makes workers feel they are part of something bigger, serving their country through Ramdev's swadeshi campaign.

Second, it makes it more difficult for employees to demand raises as the pervading seva culture make them feel selfish for asking for this.

Remember, the trouble with Brinda Karat and CITU had also begun over low wages given to factory workers in 2005. But other than the poor remunerative terms of employment there were other problems. Employees had to hand over personal cellphones when they entered the premises for work. Any infraction or wrongdoing was severely punished. 'I remember a normal, regular man went into a candy plant and ate some amla candy. Ram Bharat and his men from Haryana beat him up so much. The man came to me and stripped himself to show me his wounds – he was black, blue, red all over. I told Ram Bharat, "What are you doing? If you feel a fellow has to be punished, report him to the police! Why are you indulging in this sort of violence?"' recalls Patra.

Not that Ram Bharat, flush with the success of his brother's enterprise and at the helm of all its finances, was listening.

~

Many of the problems in the company have not gone unnoticed publicly: analysts from various leading banks around the country have visited Ramdev's factories with mixed results. Anand Shah, who works at Institutional Securities, Kotak Securities Ltd, said the team saw 'things that were not great . . . The facilities for the ghee and honey plant were not good – in terms of the hygiene standards. Even the ghee manufacturing is entirely outsourced. They only get butter from Amul and Nandini, their two major suppliers, and they only convert the butter to ghee. That's all. They don't have any back end.'

There have been problems with distributors too: less than two years after being appointed super distributors of Patanjali Ayurveda in the Bhopal, Gwalior and Jabalpur zones of Madhya Pradesh, Ram Narayan Agrawal found his super distributorship abruptly suspended. In a desperate email to Patra, beseeching him to act, Agrawal claimed that no notice was ever sent to them officially terminating the distributorship and even eight months after dispatches stopped, payments of Rs 9,46,100 were not made.

Within weeks of that, Patra received another email from Bhagwandas Mahande, a supplier in Buldhana district of Maharashtra, who claimed that after giving him an order to produce jaggery-based sugar worth Rs 22 crore for Patanjali, the company never picked up the order and drove him out of business. Like several others, he too initiated civil proceedings against Baba Ramdev and Acharya Balkrishna. Patra soon realized that these were not isolated instances, but formed a pattern of breached promises.

Patra says he himself exited the company after an extremely unpleasant face-off with Ramdev over the money that was owed to him.

'When the news spread, people began coming to me within hours that my life was in danger ... that I should leave Haridwar area immediately. Knowing what I did by then, I left,' says Patra. It marked another departure from the Patanjali fold.

Two things are clear from the string of unhappy exits from Ramdev's empire: nobody who is a threat to the power of Balkrishna and Ram Bharat ever lasts in Patanjali. And Ramdev is happy to take other people's help – but only on his own terms.

23

The Brother

Haridwar

While Ramdev's and Balkrishna's lives had been minutely examined and pored over by the UPA government after Ramdev's conflict with them, his mercurial brother Ram Bharat, riding atop the Patanjali juggernaut and in-charge of its finances, remained shadowy and fairly unknown – until his short temper landed him in trouble with the law and, despite Ramdev's best efforts, drew the spotlight on him. Confrontational and violent, his actions made a bad situation worse for Ramdev.

First, on 16 June 2010, Ram Bharat, the tall, beefy man with a handlebar moustache, lost control of his Toyota Innova and ran into two people walking on the street. An NDTV report quoted eyewitnesses claiming that a dozen vehicles from Ramdev's ashram came to the spot instantly for damage control. Ram Bharat was taken into police custody, but his victims sustained only minor injuries and the whole incident was chalked up to Ram Bharat losing control of the car due to a tyre burst.

After that first relatively minor public brush with the law, Ram Bharat landed in serious trouble three years later. On 18 October 2013, he allegedly kidnapped and tortured a former employee, Nitin Tyagi, resident of Rai village in Muzaffarnagar district of Uttar Pradesh, who had apparently stolen money and supplies worth Rs 25 lakh from the company while working there as a watchman. Tyagi alleged that Ram Bharat and four guards locked him in a room inside Patanjali Yogpeeth II for four days and tortured him. After Tyagi's grandfather filed an FIR, the police stormed the premises and rescued him. Hours after being booked for the crime, Ram Bharat absconded, triggering a statewide manhunt for him and a non-bailable warrant for his arrest.

Ever glib, Ramdev called a press conference and attacked the Congress government at the Centre and in the state for fabricating the incident and conspiring to defame him. He also asserted that his brother was not absconding and that he had not been called by the police in the first place.

Ramdev's obfuscation notwithstanding, the police investigated the case, and it seemed like the end of the road for Ram Bharat. But then the witnesses in the case mysteriously and spectacularly turned. Tyagi's grandfather, who had filed the FIR, suddenly claimed that he had done so only under police pressure. Tyagi himself signed an affidavit stating he had not been kidnapped at all. The arrest warrant was revoked and Ram Bharat was safe again. With the witness turning hostile, the Uttarakhand High Court dismissed the case on 24 December 2014.

However, this strapping man was not so lucky the next time.

About eighteen months later, in May 2015, a scuffle broke out between Patanjali staff and local truck transporters at the gate of the food park. It ended with one dead and eleven injured. Ram Bharat was caught on CCTV cameras not only instigating his security officers to attack the protesters but also indulging in violence himself, and was promptly taken into judicial custody for fourteen days. The police recovered illegal weapons – five rifles, 12 bore cartridges, gunpowder, cane shields and several lathis from the guards' room inside the food park. The guards apparently belong to Patanjali's secret private security force called the 'Bharat Sena Suraksha Bal'. In another search two days after the incident, the police recovered a sword, helmets and fifteen spears.

According to an *Indian Express* report dated 1 June 2015, the police sent two notices to the management, asking them to disclose the names and addresses of the 'personal security guards' hired by them, since the firearms and ammunition recovered from their rooms were illegal. The notice also stated that the police were in possession of a register that contained a few names of the guards under the title 'Bharat Sena Suraksha Bal'. According to Senior Superintendent of Police (Haridwar) Sweety Aggarwal, the report said, about 80 per cent of the guards were from Haryana.

When the *Express* reporter reached out to Balkrishna for a quote, he denied the presence of 'any such personal guards' and said, 'We have hired guards only from private security agencies. Since this is a 100-acre premises, there are at least 500 security guards from these agencies. They have licensed weapons. There is no question of hiring any more personal security guards. I am not even aware of this "Bharat Sena Suraksha Bal". When we have such a large contingent of security guards why would we hire any more?'

While Balkrishna brazenly denied the existence of any such security force, and the management never explained what the weapons, licensed or not, were doing on their premises in the first place, Aggarwal accused Patanjali staff of deliberately hiding evidence and said, 'We will be taking everyone involved in the clash and the cover-up into custody. Everyone involved in the cover-up will also be charged.'

In typical Ramdev style, he accused the police of

acting at the behest of their political masters – basically accusing the BJP, his allies at the time, of orchestrating the law enforcement action against him. There was no evidence of any such political conspiracy.

A week after the investigation, the police stated that it was the truck union workers who launched the first attack and also sought to charge them with attempt to murder.

Ram Bharat is still on trial at the Haridwar court as a co-accused in the case. He faces charges of criminal conspiracy and instigation to murder under section 302 of the Indian Penal Code.

24

Patanjali Ayurveda Limited

On 4 May 2017 the Patanjali group of companies doubled its revenues to Rs 10,561 crore in one year, making it the second largest FMCG company in the country, second only to Hindustan Unilever, which leads the sector with revenues of Rs 30,782 crore.

But Unilever should not be complacent. Ramdev is coming up fast, and has a new target: he promises to double revenues to Rs 20,000 crore by May 2018. In a single year Ramdev has already leapfrogged past giant companies such as ITC (Rs 10,339 crore in revenues), Nestlé India (Rs 9159 crore), Godrej Consumer Group (Rs 9134 crore), Britannia Industries (Rs 8844 crore), Dabur (Rs 7691 crore), Tata Global Beverages (Rs 6963 crore), and Marico (Rs 5918 crore). It is now far bigger than industry stalwarts Colgate–Palmolive (Rs 4010 crore), GSK Consumer Healthcare (Rs 3784 crore),

Emami (Rs 2552 crore), P&G Hygiene and Healthcare (Rs 2388 crore) and Bajaj Corp (Rs 791 crore) that have been around for several decades.

Ramdev's best-selling products included ghee, leading revenues at Rs 1467 crore, Dant Kanti toothpaste at Rs 940 crore, Ayurvedic medicines at Rs 870 crore, hair oil at Rs 825 crore and herbal soap at Rs 574 crore.

So how has this happened? Ramdev has cannibalized the market shares of the top-selling products of the blue-chip FMCG companies – in product segments that are fast-selling to begin with such as honey (top-selling Dabur product), toothpaste (top-selling Colgate product), noodles (one of Nestlé's best-sellers) and ghee (competing with Amul, Gowardhan), and carved a place for Patanjali on the shelves next to these products. Ramdev promotes most of them as 'natural' alternatives to the chemical-infused counterparts peddled by multinational corporations.

Once he is on the shelf, the high level of public recognition of him and trust in his brand propel him to the top, allowing him to skim from the multinationals, whom he indignantly brands as 'anti-national'. 'There is a certain guilt he's managed to create about buying from multinational companies, when there is a perfectly good indigenous alternative available,' says Gunendar Kapur.

At the other end of the product spectrum, where margins are not all that high, Ramdev is making a massive splash in food staples such as wheat flour, multi-grain flour and cooking oils. Promising to deliver consistent, adulteration-free quality, he has easily drawn customers away from their local baniya, or grocer, who sells unbranded produce.

Ramdev has managed to keep his prices spectacularly low for the following reasons.

First, because of cheap labour. The average Patanjali worker on the factory floor earns Rs 6000 per month for twelve-hour shifts, six days a week. As mentioned before, Ramdev terms working for Patanjali as seva for the benefit of the nation, of swadeshi, of 'Indian heritage'. The ordinary rules of the labour market don't apply here.

Second, owning two television networks has granted Ramdev a terrific advantage, keeping his advertising expenses low. In an April 2017 article, *The Economist* wrote, 'The company is able to offer customers good value partly because it spends only 2–3% of revenues on advertising [consumer firms typically spend 12–18%] … Patanjali grew by word of mouth and sells everything from detergent to cornflakes and hair oil under its own name.' But it did not just grow by word of mouth. Aastha and Sanskar take him into the living rooms of his target audience every day, all day.

Third, 'he keeps his margins low', explains Gunendar Kapur. While most multinational companies need a margin of 50 per cent to recover high advertising costs and post a 15 per cent profit (after tax), 'Ramdev's margins can be as low as 2–3 per cent', he says. 'Companies in the organized sector cannot afford to function like that.'

Last is the group's general disregard for the law.

Ramdev made a telling comment during a 'Nation-Building Meet' in Delhi in March 2013. Addressing eminent citizens, which included BJP member and eminent lawyer Ram Jethmalani, Ramdev lamented the state of the nation where it could take up to 'seven years for Tatas to get permissions'. He continued, laughing, *'Hamein to permission milti hi nahin hai . . . bina permission ke hi kaam kar rahe hain.'* (I don't get any permission at all. I am working without them.) But while Ramdev laughed as if it were a joke, the intellectual elite of Delhi were not amused. Sensing the disapproval of his audience, he tried to explain himself, *'Tata ko agar saat saal lagenge, to Baba ko to sattar saal lag jayenge. Tab tak to mein mar jaaonga!'* (If it takes the Tatas seven years to get permission, it will take Baba seventy years. By that time, I will be dead.) Ramdev laughed again, a little uncomfortably, hoping to get someone in the audience to respond with a chuckle. No one did.

That unguarded comment, so unusual for Ramdev, the master of optics, was revealing of his general disregard of legal boundaries. His long years of practice of performing for the cameras had trained him to know what to say and when to say it. For instance, on 16 April 2014, at an electoral rally, Mahant Chandnath, a candidate standing for election in Alwar, Rajasthan, leaned towards him on a rally stage and said, *'Waise kisi ne kahin se paise lani mein badi dikkat ho rahi hai . . . humare pakde bhi gaye.'* (Someone is having a lot of trouble bringing some money . . . some of ours got caught too.) Not knowing the cameras were picking up every word, Ramdev tapped his hand to stop him from speaking and whispered smilingly, *'Chup raho. Yahan baat mat karo . . . bawre ho kya? Yahan baat mat karo.'* (Keep quiet. Don't talk here. Are you crazy? Don't talk here.)

However well he may ordinarily package himself, it is well known that Ramdev's enterprise has fallen foul of the law several times. Perhaps the best and latest example of this is the case of Patanjali noodles. On 15 November 2015 Ramdev announced the launch of Patanjali noodles that he claimed were healthier – and cheaper – than Nestlé's Maggi noodles that had a market share of Rs 2000 crore. One of Nestlé's top-selling products, Maggi had run into controversy earlier that year when the Indian food standards authority said it had higher than permissible lead levels and unlabelled added MSG. Two days after their launch, Patanjali noodles ran into trouble.

The *Indian Express* reported that the Food Safety and Standards Authority of India (FSSAI) licence number 10014012000266, printed on the noodle packets, was fraudulent. On the newspaper's website was a picture of a letter written by a harassed sounding FSSAI chairperson, Ashish Bahuguna. His letter, dated 17 November 2015 and marked to FSSAI directors in charge of legal, enforcement and product approval departments, read, 'While our attention has been occupied by the Maggi case, it has been reported in the press that Patanjali have launched or are in the process of launching a new brand of noodles without obtaining proper approval for the same. Please take appropriate action in this matter.' Bahuguna also reportedly said, 'That approval was not taken. I don't know how the licence was procured.'

Then Ramdev weighed in and tried to turn the matter on its head by saying there had been some misunderstanding on the issue because the regulators 'themselves have not been able to make their own clear regulations on noodles, instant noodles'. It was impossible not to think back to his 2013 comment that he did not wait for little things like permissions.

While a *Tribune* article says the law was not clear about how Patanjali should have acquired the approvals in the first place, the FSSAI issued a show cause notice to the company demanding an explanation on 21 November 2015.

On 21 November the FSSAI issued a showcause notice to the company demanding an explanation.

But the noodle saga was to drag on. On 7 December Vinod Kumar, resident of Narwana town in Haryana, bought a packet of Ramdev's newly launched 'healthy' noodles. He cooked the noodles the next day, only to find dead worms in them. Looking inside the packet, he found worms there too.

Faced with charges he could neither duck nor bury, Ramdev screamed blue murder. At a press conference, he accused multinational consumer goods companies of conspiring against his company and hatching a plot to hurt his business – just like he did when Brinda Karat asked him uncomfortable questions. Ramdev made a lot of noise, but did not present a shred of evidence.

~

Ramdev's success has been spectacular, indeed, but it also seems tentative. Fundamental questions linger about his products. In December 2016 the Haridwar district court slapped a fine of Rs 11 lakh on Patanjali Ayurveda for misleading advertising and passing off products manufactured by others as their own. But such deception is nothing new. Ramdev has being doing so, according to Haridwar residents, from the days when he first set up his 'clinic' under Balkrishna in Shankar Dev's Kripalu Bagh Ashram.

On 18 April 2017 the *Indian Express* reported that the Food and Drug Administration of Haryana had found Patanjali 'cow ghee' to be 'substandard and unsafe'. They had conducted the tests in October 2016 and revealed their reports only in response to an RTI filed by the newspaper. Any other company would have been scrambling to do damage control and recalling products from the market. In May 2015, when Nestlé's Maggi noodles were dubbed 'unsafe and substandard' because of the presence of MSG and lead in it, Nestlé responded with a recall of products worth Rs 320 crore, an apology to its consumers, and a reiteration that the company wanted to make safe products for its customers. In other words, the company took responsibility for the situation. On the other hand, Ramdev seemed to have no intention of accepting responsibility.

A *Mint* article reported that a Patanjali spokesperson had scoffed that the report 'did not make sense' because the existing standards set by FSSAI 'are based on available products and not cow ghee. Contents in cow ghee are different from the ghee other companies sell. We are the first company to bring cow ghee in commercial market. There is no standard for cow ghee ... so it does not make sense.' Patanjali had decided to brazen it out.

The spokesperson's comments do not respond to the charges that their product was found to be 'substandard and unsafe'. Instead he lied: the fact is that several other companies do produce cow ghee – Gowardhan, Mother Dairy, Anik, Madhusudan, Milkfood, Healthaid, Gopaljee Ananda, Nestlé, Britannia and Amul. And, finally, can the company that procures tens of thousands of tonnes of white butter a year from millions of milk producers around the country be completely sure that their ghee is 'cow ghee' at all? The simple reality is that there *is* a standard for ghee – cow ghee or otherwise – and in April 2017 Patanjali's ghee failed to meet it.

A week later, on 24 April 2017, the *Economic Times* reported that the Canteen Stores Department (CSD), selling 5300 products to 12 million consumers serving in or veterans of India's defence forces, suspended the sale of Patanjali Ayurveda's amla juice from their 3901 stores. It had done so after the Central Food Laboratory in Kolkata tested samples and deemed it 'unfit for consumption'.

The company's official response was classic Patanjali: they claimed that since amla juice is a medicinal product, it should have been tested according to the standards of the ministry of ayush, and not the FSSAI regulations. Yet, common sense suggests that the rules governing medicinal products are likely more stringent than rules governing food products.

These are only three instances of Ramdev running into trouble with the regulators. There have been many others, including six run-ins with the Advertising Standards Council of India for unsubstantiated and misleading advertising.

Experts say that a company cannot grow at such a pace without having issues of this kind. The problem is not just the fact that there are such issues. It is how the company chooses to respond to allegations of any kind that is troubling – counter-allegations of unfair tests, and conspiracy and foul play.

~

Despite these constant question marks over Patanjali products, Indians continue to place their trust in the company. Their faith in the saffron-robed Ramdev remains intact because he repeatedly, self-assuredly and charmingly reassures them that he, in the great tradition of Hindu sadhus, is running this company as a service to the nation. 'I sleep on the floor, I am a fakir ... all the profits are going to charity. I don't own anything in my name ... don't trust the multinationals or stooges of other corporations who defame me. They are doing so because they cannot stand the success of Patanjali.'

In the end, Patanjali has been a powerful disruptor,

a true game changer for Indian consumers. Ramdev has reinvented the rules of the game. He has expanded and deepened the market in places that no one else had noticed before. A new consumer from the lower middle classes is in the market who perhaps cannot afford the expensive products of the MNCs, but can buy Baba Ramdev's products at a cheaper price. There are others from various other classes of society who buy his products because their 'swadeshi' nature appeals to their Indian spirit.

Yet, the advantage of the first mover is beginning to wane for Patanjali. The corporates and other babas are coming into his domain. Colgate has launched a herbal toothpaste. Unilever bought an Ayurvedic hair oil company (Indulekha) and is doing test-runs for its own Ayurveda brand, Ayush, in south India. Dabur is reinventing itself and its packaging along with other Indian companies, readying to duel with Patanjali for the swadeshi turf.

Other less controversial godmen have taken notes too. Sri Sri Ravi Shankar has launched his own 'Divine Shop' that produces premium health supplements, honey, coconut oils, green gram, a non-fluoride toothpaste called Sudanta and cosmetics. Sadhguru Jaggi Vasudev's Isha store sells Ayurvedic and siddha medicines, food supplements and a cosmetic 'snanam powder' that promises to control body odour and prevent skin ailments. Even though they do not offer half as many products, both their websites are more refined and attractive than the Patanjali website – a clear signal that their target audiences may come from a different social strata.

Ramdev has come a long way, protected by his orange robes and all that they signify to believing Hindus. He may have come this far by not paying attention to boundaries, but he will not be able to go further without playing by the rules. He is too visible, too big now to take risks. Already in the villages of Haryana, he is popularly known as Lala Ramdev, lala being a derogatory term for a businessman.

With other godmen also getting into the game, there is no doubt that they will raise the bar, that the protection of saffron he has relied on will be less effective. Ramdev needs to be ready for this.

25

Conclusion

My search for the people who had worked with Ramdev, who were presumably inspired by him, his vision and his empire, was interesting and rewarding. Of course, I found many who were energized and motivated by Ramdev and his story. But the man also leaves behind a trail of a different sort.

A trail of people whose goodwill or frailties he used to further his own enrichment and pursue his own agenda, people who were left by the wayside after they had served their purpose. A trail of people who either vanished into thin air, or died mysterious deaths, or live on in utter fear of him. A trail of decisions and political machinations driven not by the principles he espouses but by expediency. A trail blazing into the post-truth world where reality was mutable and the trusting millions who believe in him could be manipulated through his television channels. Finally, a trail of shirked responsibility. For every negative event surrounding him, he has consistently yelled foul, always choosing to lay the blame at someone else's door – the government's or his detractors', accusing them of conspiring against him and fabricating evidence to pull him down. On some occasions, he may have even been right, but he has overused the argument to such an extent that it has lost its credibility.

All Ramdev's former allies, aides, supporters and mentors who had watched him rise but had fallen by the wayside at some point seemed to have been waiting for a call like mine, from anyone at all, asking them about their time with Ramdev. They were all ready to tell their stories.

Yet for all the dubious choices he has made since his rise to fame and fortune, no one can take away or belittle the legacy of this farmer's son. Ramdev took yoga and Ayurveda out of the restrictive realm of religion and made it an accessible practice of preventive health care for millions of Indians. He reminded them that the pursuit of spirituality has little meaning if the body is unhealthy. Even today, despite the pressures of running a growing business, he continues to hold yoga camps in Haridwar. He's still on television every day, thanks to a combination of reruns and fresh shoots.

Conclusion

Most important, he drew attention to India's own health care heritage – Ayurveda. Leaving aside how it was all executed, Ramdev's charisma reminded people that not every ailment needs a modern doctor. There are other options that are less intrusive.

Today, preventive health care is the new buzzword for the health-care industry globally. Prevention is better than cure may be an old adage, but India's beleaguered 60-billion-dollar health-care industry, groaning and creaking under the staggering pressure of 1.2 billion people, is recognizing the worth of that ancient wisdom now. Ramdev has undoubtedly played a vital role in making Ayurveda and yoga relevant and accessible to millions of Indians.

In pursuit of that goal of offering healthy living options to the market, his astute business instinct has also spawned India's fastest-growing company. The sheer speed of growth of his company and the breathtaking ambition of it as he chases another impossible-sounding target of doubling revenues to Rs 20,000 crore in 2017–18 will always inspire entrepreneurs. Whatever the future may bring for Patanjali, young people without degrees and money will draw inspiration from its dazzling ascent. The tales of how a homegrown company shook up multinational corporations out of a stupor, forced them to change their strategy, take notice of Ayurveda as a source of new products will also endure.

Nothing can take this legacy away from Ramdev. It is his to keep.

While Ramdev's legacy relating to television, Ayurveda, yoga and business is fairly clear, what is his political legacy? Every venture he has touched in his life has been a success but popular opinion may suggest that he failed in his political ambition.

Ramdev strayed into politics accidentally, not by design. After he met Rajeev Dixit, it just sort of happened: he tried to harness his fame as a sadhu-cum-yoga-teacher to propel himself on to a larger platform and dreamt of his own political party. But somewhere along the way Ramdev seems to have decided against trying to become a mainstream political player and instead use his political power – and it is undeniably clear that he does have political power thanks to his popularity among people – to further his business interests. Ramdev's politics now plays a supporting role for his business empire – and that's not a failure as much as a sensible, pragmatic realignment.

But pragmatism and taking utilitarian, hard-boiled decisions is second nature for Ramdev. It is easy to forget that Ramdev was not always a BJP ally. Once upon a time he was the protégé of the Congress, willing to hijack the VHP–RSS agenda to hand over a victory to

Conclusion

allies in the Grand Old Party. Without his old Congress allies, and their largesse – land discounts, permissions, loan approvals – Ramdev could not have become as powerful as he had in the first place. Yet when he realized the Congress was a sinking ship and fell out with his earlier godfathers, he negotiated a safe landing space with the VHP–RSS–BJP combine.

Smoothly, courageously, he abandoned the Congress party, becoming part of the battering ram that brought it down. Ramdev is said to have helped the BJP with the 2014 general election campaign and is now apparently reaping rewards for that service. In May 2017, a Reuters article alleged that according to (unpublished) documents examined by them, Ramdev has received 46 million dollars in land allocations and discounts from BJP-led state governments.

But do not take this to be a permanent realignment. Ramdev is a hardheaded ally who can blow hot and cold at will.

Today, even as he reiterates his support for the BJP government, Ramdev is quietly mending fences with his former allies-turned-foes, holding public and private meetings with Lalu Prasad Yadav, Akhilesh and Mulayam Singh Yadav and the Congress politicians. If he ever needs to abandon the BJP, his old alliances may well be restored enough to make the transition possible.

Ramdev's ability to nurse new dreams, pursue them

and abandon them if needed, his fluidity, makes it impossible to categorize his political flirtation as a complete failure. His ability to adapt and respond to changing landscapes is formidable – and admirable. When denied political domination, he chose to harness politics to seek economic dominion.

Yet, Ramdev and the empire he has built now stand at a crossroads. However beguiling it is to believe in the fairy tale of one man's ability to build an empire from nothing in almost no time, his success is far from assured.

A seething rivalry between his brother and his deputy threatens his empire. Ram Bharat and Balkrishna, who always banded together against any third ascending power in Ramdev's empire, do not enjoy a close relationship. One gets the impression that for Ramdev blood is thicker than water and so Balkrishna, given to insecurity and jealousy, has long been envious of Ram Bharat – for instance, all those years ago, when Karamveer was still around, Balkrishna was upset with Ramdev for buying Ram Bharat a bike and a house.

These two men have long been Ramdev's lieutenants, executing his orders on the ground. Ram Bharat has always been in charge of the purse strings. Balkrishna oversees the Ayurveda and to lesser extent the FMCG side of the empire, under Ramdev's watchful eye.

But Balkrishna, a man who knows everything about Ramdev, is also seen to be attention-hungry and desires

Conclusion

a prominent public profile, like Ramdev's – that's why he is so active on social media, building his own brand, even making claims of discovering the mythical sanjeevani buti, the herb described in the Ramayana as one that can raise the dead to life. Ramdev and Balkrishna's shared history apparently forced Ramdev's hand to give him space on the masthead of the company and on their advertisements.

But don't be fooled into thinking they're equals. Balkrishna is without a doubt Ramdev's pliable and controllable deputy. It was nothing but expediency that led Ramdev to put 94 per cent of Patanjali in Balkrishna's name – his long-standing subordinate could be controlled as neither Ramdev nor his family could sit at the helm without a backlash.

It is generally speculated that Ram Bharat is not particularly thrilled with this arrangement. Yet, because he continues to control the finances of the company, he is mollified. This division of real and perceived power keeps their rivalries from spilling over. For now.

But it is hard not to feel as though this house of cards may come crashing down.

For Ramdev, the stakes have never been higher. And there are some questions he needs to consider. Will he find the courage to distance his unpredictable family, particularly his brother, from the company? Will he be able to stand up to people within his organization and prevent them from pursuing unfair trade practices with his distributors and suppliers? Can he rein in his advertising juggernaut from misleading and mis-selling to the public? Is he willing to own the mistakes made in the past and correct them? Most important, is he willing to play by the rules of the society he lives in and hold himself up to the laws that ordinary businessmen have to adhere to? Is he ready to stop using his saffron robes as a holy shield against public scrutiny?

Ramdev will need every ounce of his formidable imagination and famed stubbornness to fix his mistakes and take the hard calls needed to make Patanjali Ayurveda Limited a truly world-class organization. If he does do so, his dream of spawning an Indian multinational company could well transform into reality.

If not, it will remain just that. A dream.

Sources

Chapter 1: The Tycoon

Interviews with:
Aditya Pittie, Abneesh Roy, S.K. Patra, Harish Bijoor, K.K. Mishra and Sandeep Dev.

External Sources
1. 'India's Baba Ramdev Billionaire Is Not Baba Ramdev', Megha Bahree, *Forbes*, 26 October 2016.
   https://www.forbes.com/sites/meghabahree/ 2016/10/26/indias-baba-ramdev-billionaire-is-not-baba-ramdev/#352aaa272d2e
2. 'India's Craze for Ayurveda Is Producing Billionaires', Preetika Rana, *Wall Street Journal*, India Real Time Blog, 16 September 2016.
   https://blogs.wsj.com/indiarealtime/2016/09/16/indias-craze-for-ayurveda-is-producing-billionaires/
3. http://www.barcindia.co.in/statistic.aspx
4. 'Diet Pepsi Is a Toilet Cleaner, Throw Them Out: Baba Ramdev', ET Now, edited excerpts, 15 November 2016.
   http://economictimes.indiatimes.com/industry/cons-products/fmcg/diet-pepsi-is-a-toilet-cleaner-throw-them-out-baba-ramdev/articleshow/55437289.cms
5. 'Anti-capitalism Yoga Guru Baba Ramdev Has a Major Brand in India', Preeti Khurana, 2 January 2016.

http://www.theaustralian.com.au/business/wall-street-journal/anticapitalism-yoga-guru-baba-ramdev-has-a-major-brand-in-india/news-story/00fd86cf2eaf18b05a46fa535e0ebccc

6. 'Patanjali Will Shut the Gate in Colgate, Make Nestlés Bird Disappear: Baba Ramdev', *Economic Times*, 30 April 2016.
http://economictimes.indiatimes.com/industry/cons-products/fmcg/patanjali-will-shut-the-gate-in-colgate-make-nestles-bird-disappear-baba-ramdev/articleshow/52024817.cms

7. Ramdev Promises to Make MNCs Do 'Sirshasana'
https://www.youtube.com/watch?v= PNLYKG2Q7Bc
Published by *Economic Times*, 28 April 2016.

8. 'Baba Ramdev's Patanjali Home Worship Products Will Hit Stores in the Next Two Months', Ratna Bhushan and Sambhavi Anand, *Economic Times*, 26 August 2016.
http://timesofindia.indiatimes.com/business/india-business/Baba-Ramdevs-Patanjali-home-worship-products-will-hit-stores-in-the-next-two-months/articleshow/53867847.cms

9. 'Patanjali Plans to Launch "Swadeshi" Jeans', Vivek Deshpande, *Indian Express*, 10 October 2016.
http://indianexpress.com/article/india/india-news-india/patanjali-plans-to-launch-swadeshi-jeans-3026282/

10. 'Fati hui jeans hai fashion', Baba Ramdev talks of ripped jeans
https://www.youtube.com/watch?v= UuZ14GIFNWI
Published by Bharat Swabhiman Samachar, 9 November 2015.

11. Ramdev launches 'swadeshi' jeans and expounds Patanjali expansion plans
https://www.youtube.com/watch?v=-BLI7jZwbBM
Published by ABP News, 11 September 2016.

Chapter 2: The Boy Ramdev

Interviews with:
Devdutt Yadav, Acharya Abhaydev, Acharya Balkrishna, Gulabo Devi, Acharya Bramhadev and Sandeep Dev.

Sources

External Sources
1. http://www.census2011.co.in/census/district/223-mahendragarh.html
2. Sandeep Dev, *Ek Yogi, Ek Yoddha* (Delhi: Bloomsbury, 2015).
3. 'Making of Brand Baba', Varghese K. George and Charu Suda Kasturi, *Hindustan Times*, 12 June 2011.
   http://www.hindustantimes.com/india/making-of-brand-baba/story-C8fWFh0bKDIhmtRcgsoIfI.html

Chapter 3: The Deputy and the Mentor

Interviews with:
Karamveer Maharaj, Acharya Balkrishna, Vipin Pradhan, Ishwar Bharadwaj, Sushant Mahendru, Sandeep Dev, Acharya Abhaydev, Surakshit Goswami and local residents of Kankhal.

External Sources
1. 'Billionaire Baba', Damyani Datta and Piyush Babele, *India Today*, 10 June 2011.
   http://indiatoday.intoday.in/story/baba-ramdev-empire-success-as-yoga-guru-in-haridwar/1/141099.html

Chapter 4: The Guru

Interviews with:
Karamveer Maharaj, Vipin Pradhan, Professor Ishwar Bharadwaj, Gulabo Devi, Sushant Mahendru, Surakshit Goswami and Acharya Bramhadev.

External Sources
1. About the ashram where the three began making chawanprash in the early to mid 1990s
   http://tripurayogashram.blogspot.in/2011/06/introduction-about-swami-ji.html
2. Copy of the deed forming the Divya Yog Mandir Trust, 5 January 1995, in Kankhal, Haridwar

Sources

Chapter 5: The Early Days

Interviews with:
Karamveer Maharaj, Acharya Balkrishna, Vipin Pradhan, Dr Veena Shastri, Baba Ramdev, Sharad Kumar Gupta, Tarun Kumar, Manoj Khanna, Dr Ghosh, Radhika Nagrath and Devdutt Yadav.

External Sources
1. 'And Then There Will Be a Revolution', Priyanka P. Narain, *Mint*, 5 April 2009.
   http://www.livemint.com/Politics/BtLE0nBloRrgvQuW9rD6XJ/8216And-then-there-will-be-a-revolution8217.html
2. 'From Bicycle to Jet Plane. Baba Ramdev's Smashing Success', Rohit, CNN ireport, 21 June 2011.
   http://ireport.cnn.com/docs/DOC-624778
3. Sandeep Dev, *Ek Yogi, Ek Yoddha* (Delhi: Bloomsbury, 2015).

Chapter 6: Aastha Television

Interviews with:
Madhav Kant Mishra, Kirit Mehta, Neena Mehta, Dilip Kabra and long-time employees of Aastha.

External Sources
1. SEBI press release, 6 September 2005. http://www.watchoutinvestors.com/Press_Release/sebi/2005115.ASP?cntrl_no=COMP1892
2. 'The Origins of Ramdev', Rahul Bhatia, *Open* magazine, 2 July 2011.
   http://www.openthemagazine.com/article/india/the-origins-of-ramdev
3. Sebi order dated 9 September 2005 barring Aastha Broadcasting Network Limited from dealing in securities and accessing capital markets till 14 January 2007. http://www.watchoutinvestors.com/Press_Release/sebi/2005115.ASP?cntrl_no=COMP1892

Sources

4. Securities Appellate Tribunal order in *Sebi vs Shri Ajit Satyaprakash Gupta* dated 7 June 2006 upholding Sebi's order barring Aastha Broadcasting Network Limited from dealing in securities and accessing capital markets till 14 January 2007.
   https://indiankanoon.org/doc/762798/?type=print

Chapter 7: The TV Star

Interviews with:
Madhav Kant Mishra, Kirit Mehta and Dilip Kabra.

External Sources
1. The Science of Yoga, *Time* magazine cover, 23 April 2001.
   https://www.amazon.com/Magazine-April-Christy-Turlington-Science/dp/B00BAW36ZS
2. 'The Power of Yoga', Richard Corliss, *Time* magazine, 15 April 2001.
   http://content.time.com/time/health/article/ 0,8599,106356,00.html
3. Madonna on Oprah, talking about how Yoga centred her (1998)
   https://www.youtube.com/watch?v=iTKo7qspFDU (Madonna on Yoga)
   Published by Cispera Espera, 11 April 2012
4. 'Look at This Man's Body: This Is What Yoga Can Do', Deirdre Donahue, *USA Today*, 24 April 2002.
   https://usatoday30.usatoday.com/life/books/2002/2002-04-24-rodney-yee.htm
5. 'Consumer Attitudes towards Spiritual Quest of Religious Channels in Delhi/NCR Region', Anagha Shukre, Research Paper, Bvimsr.com, 11 November 2011.
   http://www.bvimsr.com/documents/publication/ 2009V1N2/11.pdf

Sources

Chapter 8: Friends in High Places

Interviews with:
Baba Ramdev, Acharya Balkrishna, Karamveer Maharaj, Vipin Pradhan, Jitender Rana and Manoj Rawat.

External Sources
1. Divya Pharmacy licence with N.P. Singh's signature – 1995, Haridwar.
2. 'When the G in NGO Stands for Governor, There Is a Problem', Raghvendra Rao, *Indian Express*, 7 May 2006.
   http://archive.indianexpress.com/news/when-g-in-ngo-stands-for-governor-there-is-a-problem--------/3946/0
3. 'Baba Ramdev's Epic Swindle', Manoj Rawat and Mahipal Kunwar, *Tehelka*, 19 March 2012.
   http://archive.tehelka.com/story_main52.asp?filename=Ws190312 Black_money.asp
4. SEBI's 'Watch Out Investors' against Yogi Pharmacy
   http://www.watchoutinvestors.com/history.asp?def_code=C0034432
5. 'Yogi Pharmacy Barred from Accessing the Capital Markets', *Indian Express*, 5 December 1998.
   http://expressindia.indianexpress.com/fe/daily/19981205/33955604.html
6. Yogi Pharmacy delisting among delisted company names. Delisting.in, 14 June 2004.
   http://www.delisting.in/list_of_delisted_companies.php?sf=y&type=c&frdate=&todate=&sel_year=
7. 'Governor Sudershan Agrawal inaugurates Patanjali Yog Peeth Trust', Sulekha, 6 August 2006.
   http://creative.sulekha.com/aim-of-baba-ramdev-the-yoga-guru_383725_blog
8. 'The Messiah of Yoga: Governor Inaugurated Patanjali Yog Peeth II', Mansi Agarwal, Lifepositive.com, July 2006.
   https://www.lifepositive.com/the-messiah-of-yoga/
9. Ramdev attends engagement ceremony of Rajat Prakash, son of

Sources

Renu Prakash and O.P. Srivastava. Pictures with Subrato and Svapna Roy, Nitisha Kashyap, *Times of India*, 13 November 2013.
10. Pictures of Baba Ramdev with the Roy and Srivastava families. http://photogallery.indiatimes.com/events/delhi/rajat-shvetas-engagement-ceremony/articleshow/25756987.cms
11. 'O.P. Srivastava's Role as Baba Ramdev's Financial Advisor to Be Explored', *Tribune*, 11 June 2011. http://www.tribuneindia.com/2011/20110612/main1.htm

Chapter 9: Mystery 1 – The Ally's Murder

FIR filed in Kankhal Thana on 27 December 2004 for Yogananda's murder.
Closure report on Yogananda's murder case filed on 25 October 2005 by B.B. Juyal.

Chapter 10: A New Mentor Enters

Interviews with:
K.N. Govindacharya, Ram Bahadur Rai, Rajeev Dixit and Pradeep Dixit.

External Sources
1. http://rajivdixit.net/
2. http://rajivdixitbooks.blogspot.co.uk

Chapter 11: The Old Mentor Exits

Interviews with:
Madhav Kant Mishra, Karamveer Maharaj, Vipin Pradhan, Sushant Mahendru, Dr Ghosh, Professor Ishwar Bharadwaj and Gulabo Devi.

External Sources
1. 'Ramdev Spreading Nepotism: Baba Karamveer', Webindia.com, 12 April 2011.
http://news.webindia123.com/news/articles/India/20110413/1728794.html

Sources

Chapter 12: The Seeds of an Empire

Interviews with:

K.K. Pittie, Ishwar Bharadwaj, Madhav Kant Mishra, Kirit Mehta, Bhakti Mehta, Neena Mehta, Subodh Kant Sahay, Tarun Kumar, Sunil Pandey, Manoj Khanna and Veena Shastri.

External Sources

1. 'Non-bailable Warrant against Subrata Roy Cancelled after He Appears in Court', Mustafa Shaikh, *India Today*, 21 April 2017. http://indiatoday.intoday.in/story/sahara-subrata-roy-sebi-nbw/1/934791.html
2. 'O.P. Srivastava's Role as Baba Ramdev's Financial Advisor to Be Explored', *Tribune*, 11 June 2011. http://www.tribuneindia.com/2011/20110612/main1.htm
3. Acharya Balkrishna's profile on their official website http://www.acharyabalkrishna.com/profile/patanjali-yogpeeth/
4. http://www.fssai.gov.in/home/fss-legislation/food-safety-and-standards-act.html
5. 'Boom Time for Yoga', Varun Verma, *Telegraph*, 15 January 2006. https://www.telegraphindia.com/1060115/asp/look/story_5705374.asp
6. 'Save Your Breath', Namrata Joshi, *Outlook* magazine, 23 January 2006. http://www.outlookindia.com/magazine/story/save-your-breath/229910
7. K.K. Pittie's profile. Pooja Mujumdar, *Marwar* magazine, 8 December 2015. http://www.marwar.com/people/profile/a-man-for-all-seasons.html

Chapter 13: Enter Brinda Karat

Interviews with:

Brinda Karat and Veena Shastri.

Sources

External Sources

1. 'How the Karat-Ramdev War Began', Sma Kazime, Express News Service, 7 January 2006.
   http://archive.is/WG6tI
   http://vande-maatharam.blogspot.in/2006/01/how-karat-ramdev-war-began.html
2. 'In the Name of Ayurveda', T.K. Rajalakshmi, *Frontline*, 28 January 2006.
   http://www.frontline.in/navigation/?type=static&page=flonnet&rdurl=fl2302/stories/200602 10002604200.htm
3. 'Sacked Workers Open Swami Ramdev's Bag of Bones', Kay Benedict, *DNA*, 7 January 2006.
   http://www.dnaindia.com/india/report-sacked-workers-open-swami-ramdev-s-bag-of-bones-1006211
4. 'Fewer Rational Thinkers Today' (interview with Brinda Karat), T.K. Rajalakshmi, *Frontline*, 4 October 2013.
   http://www.frontline.in/cover-story/fewer-rational-thinkers-today/article5137397.ece
5. 'Yogi Cleared of Animal Parts Row', BBC News, 8 March 2006.
   http://news.bbc.co.uk/2/hi/south_asia/4786114.stm
6. 'Workers Struggle in Divya Pharmacy: A Report and Full Text of Press Conference', *People's Democracy*, Vol. XXX, No. 3, 15 January 2006.
   http://archives.peoplesdemocracy.in/2006/0115/01152006_brinda.htm

Chapter 14: Patanjali Is Born

External Sources
1. ROC documents forming PAL Haridwar, 13 January 2006.

Chapter 15: The Yoga Roadshow

Interviews with:
Kirit Mehta, Bhakti Mehta, Neena Mehta, Madav Kant Mishra and Arvind Joshi.

Sources

External Sources

1. 'Swami Ramdev Wins UK Award', PTI, *Times of India*, 14 July 2006.
   http://timesofindia.indiatimes.com/world/rest-of-world/Swami-Ramdev-wins-UK-award/articleshow/1749400.cms?prtpage=1
2. 'Lord Paul, Swami Ramdev Honoured in London', Rediff India Abroad, 14 July 2006.
   http://www.rediff.com/news/2006/jul/14award.htm
3. 'Ramdev Awarded in UK, Meets Queen', *Indian Express*, 14 July 2006.
   http://archive.indianexpress.com/news/ramdev-awarded-in-uk-meets-queen/171401/
4. 'Ramdev Promotes Yoga in UK', *Organizer*, 3 September 2006.
   http://organiser.org/archives/historic/dynamic/modules41ba.html?name=Content&pa=showpage&pid=147&page=34
5. http://www.yogapranayama.com/credentials
6. Resolution of an extraordinary meeting of shareholders of Vedic Aarogya Pvt. Ltd dated 21 May 2007, filed with the Registrar of Companies.

Chapter 16: Mystery 2 – The Guru's Disappearance

Interviews with:

Acharya Karamveer, Acharya Balkrishna, Sushant Mahendru, Ishwar Bharadwaj, Vipin Pradhan, Sunil Pandey, residents of Haridwar, Manoj Khanna and Radhika Nagrath.

External Sources

1. 'Ramdev to Hold Yoga Camps on US Visit', Dharam Shourie, *DNA*, 10 May 2007.
   http://www.dnaindia.com/world/report-ramdev-to-hold-yoga-camps-on-us-visit-1095894
2. Swami Ramdev speaks about guru's disappearance. Bharatswabhiman Samachar, 15 October 2013.
   https://www.youtube.com/watch?v=Ssl6gyXSOUk

Sources

3. 'Shankar Dev Leaves Ashram due to "Unbearable Pain"', One India, 19 July 2007.
   http://www.oneindia.com/2007/07/19/baba-ramdevs-guru-leaves-ashram-due-to-unbearable-pain-1184846062.html
4. 'If the Pose Holds', Sannjay Rawat, Pushp Sharma
   http://www.outlookindia.com/magazine/story/if-the-pose-holds/282475
5. 'Swami Ramdev Raises Funds in US for University', Rediff.com, 24 July 2007.
   http://www.rediff.com/news/report/ramdev/20070724.htm
6. 'British House of Commons Honours Yoga Guru Ramdev', One India, 18 July 2007.
   http://www.oneindia.com/2007/07/18/british-house-of-commons-honours-yoga-guru-ramdev-1184769558.html
7. FIR filed by Balkrishna on 17 July 2007 on Shankar Dev's disappearance.
8. Reply of CBI (Delhi) to an RTI query on the Shankar Dev disappearance case.
9. Reply of CBI (Dehradun) to an RTI query on the Shankar Dev disappearance case.

Chapter 17: The Reinvention

Interviews with:
Pranav Pandya, Sunil Pandey, Pradeep Dixit, Rajeev Dixit, Ashok Tripathi and Baba Ramdev.

External Sources
1. Timeline from the official site of the Ganga Raksha Munch
   https://translate.google.co.in/translate?hl= en&sl=hi&u=http://gangarakshamunch.com/Andolan.aspx&prev=search
2. 'Ramdev's Ganga Mission Brings VHP, Muslim Clerics Together', IANS, Twocircles.net, 19 September 2008.
   http://twocircles.net/2008sep19/ramdevs_ganga_mission_brings_vhp_muslim_clerics_together.html

3. 'Kanpur Tanneries Earn It Title of Worst Polluter', Priyanka P. Narain, *Mint*, 26 September 2008.
   http://www.livemint.com/Politics/PAD9GKTO1t7N65tNnTNECO/Kanpur8217s-tanneries-earn-it-title-of-the-worst-polluter.html
4. 'PM Promises Cabinet Meet Soon on Ganga Cleanup Plans', One India News, 20 September 2008.
   http://www.oneindia.com/2008/09/20/pm-promises-cabinet-meet-soon-on-ganga-clean-up-plans-1221914104.html
5. 'Ganga Declared National River', *Indian Express*, 5 November 2008.
   http://archive.indianexpress.com/news/ganga-declared-national-river/381554/

Chapter 18: The Aastha Takeover

Interviews with:
Kirit Mehta, Bhakti Mehta, Neena Mehta and Chetan Mehta.

External Sources
1. 'The Origins of Ramdev', Rahul Bhatia, *Open* magazine, 2 July 2011.
   www.openthemagazine.com/article/india/the-origins-of-ramdev
2. A copy of Kirit Mehta's letter resigning as chairman and managing director of Aastha Broadcasting Network Limited dated 13 November 2009, filed with the Registrar of Companies.
3. Securities Appellate Tribunal judgment in *Sebi vs Cheneena Impex Pvt. Ltd. and Ors.* dated 19 January 2007 permanently freezing 97 per cent of Aastha Broadcasting Network Limited shares.
   https://indiankanoon.org/doc/1050207/
4. A copy of the Aastha Broadcasting Network Limited board resolution appointing Shiv Kumar Garg as chairman and executive additional director, filed with the Registrar of Companies on 20 November 2009.

Sources

Chapter 19: Mystery 3 – The Mentor's Sudden Death

Interviews with:
Madan Dubey, Ram Bahadur Rai, Roopesh Pandey, Pradeep Dixit, Ved Prakash Vaidik and Pranav Pandya.

External Sources
1. K.K. Pittie's profile. Pooja Mujumdar, *Marwar* magazine, 8 December 2015.
   http://www.marwar.com/people/profile/a-man-for-all-seasons.html
2. 'And Then, There Will Be a Revolution', Priyanka P. Narain, *Mint*, 5 April 2009.
   http://www.livemint.com/Politics/BtLE0n BloRrgvQuW9r D6XJ/8216And-then-there-will-be-a-revolution8217.html
3. 'Baba Ramdev Launches Political Party Named Bharat Swabhiman', *DNA*, 17 March 2010.
   http://www.dnaindia.com/india/report-baba-ramdev-launches-political-party-named-bharat-swabhiman-1359967
4. 'Baba Ramdev's Bharat Nirman Yatra Kicks Off from Dwarka', *Desh Gujarat*, 3 September 2010.
   http://deshgujarat.com/2010/09/03/baba-ramdevs-bharat-nirman-yatra-kicks-off-from-gujarats-dwarka/
5. Ramdev and Rajeev Dixit speaking together to Bharat Swabhiman Andolan volunteers.
   https://www.youtube.com/watch?v=IPBVWSC dbOw
   Published by Rajiv Dixit, 24 July 2009.
6. Rajeev Dixit's last lecture at Bemetara, three hours before his collapse in a locked bathroom on 29 November 2010
   https://www.youtube.com/watch?v=ikBHLybjTaw
   Published by Rajiv Dixit's official website, 5 April 2012.
7. Ramdev asserts that he talked to Dixit on phone for an hour after heart attack and Madan Dubey's public statement demanding postmortem
   https://www.youtube.com/watch?v=3aBs0BOK rxI&t=46s

Sources

8. Ramdev asserts he spoke to Rajeev Dixit for an hour before death, exhorting him to accept allopathic line of treatment to save his life. He also asserts that Rajeev Dixit had diabetes, blood pressure and heart ailments, all genetic problems
https://www.youtube.com/watch?v=J-BmL7x6Fjk
Published by Rajiv Dixit's official website, 5 April 2010.
9. Ramdev alleges Congress conspiracy in trying to frame him in Rajeev Dixit's death and Shankar Dev's disappearance https://www.youtube.com/watch?v=0oZXJ2GplsE
Published by Indian Politics, 6 January 2014.
10. Dixit's followers question Baba Ramdev after Rajeev Dixit's death
https://www.youtube.com/watch?v=HysZIDJdY34
Published by Yogesh Mishra, Sanatan Gyan Peeth, 26 September 2016.
11. 'RSS Rejected Ramdev Project to Revive BJP, Says Book', Rasheed Kidwai, *Telegraph*, 20 June 2016 (the book is *Gurus: Stories of India's Leading Babas* by Bhavdeep Kang).
https://www.telegraphindia.com/1160620/jsp/nation/story_92222.jsp
12. http://rajivdixitmp3.com

Chapter 20: The Anna Movement

Interviews with:
K.N. Govindacharya, Ram Bahadur Rai, Madhav Kant Mishra, Ved Prakash Vaidik, Pradeep Dixit and Subodh Kant Sahay.

External Sources
1. 'Some Telephone Conversations', *Open* magazine, 20 November 2010.
http://www.openthemagazine.com/article/india/some-telephone-conversations
2. 'The Satyam Scandal: How India's Biggest Corporate Fraud Unfolded', Manu Balachandran, Quartz India, 9 April 2015.
https://qz.com/379877/the-satyam-scandal-how-indias-biggest-corporate-fraud-unfolded/

Sources

3. 'Timeline of Team Anna's Jan Lokpal Agitation', PTI, India TV News, 24 July 2011.
   http://www.indiatvnews.com/politics/national/timeline-of-team-anna-s-jan-lokpal-agitation-5238.html
4. 'Indian Activist Anna Hazare Begins Anti-graft Fast', BBC News, 5 April 2011.
   http://www.bbc.com/news/world-south-asia-12968151
5. 'Thousands Protest against Corruption', David Lalmalsawma, Reuters, 5 April 2011.
   http://in.reuters.com/article/idINIndia- 56135720110405
6. 'Anna Hazare's Fast Has Inspired Millions of Indians', Chetan Bhagat, *Guardian*, 17 August 2011.
   https://www.theguardian.com/world/2011/aug/17/anna-hazare-arrest-inspired-indians
7. Lokpal Bill: Ramdev backs Hazare
   http://indiatoday.intoday.in/video/lokpal-bill-ramdev-backs-anna-hazare/1/134675.html
8. 'Baba Ramdev Roots for Anna Hazare', PTI, 8 April 2011.
   http://www.business-standard.com/article/economy-policy/baba-ramdev-roots-for-anna-hazare-111040800211_1.html
9. Ramdev on Anna Hazare's stage
   https://www.youtube.com/watch?v= IAq6ZCKVLaA
   Published by TV9 Gujarati, 8 April 2011.
10. 'First Meeting of Lokpal Bill Drafting Panel', *Economic Times*, 26 April 2011.
    http://economictimes.indiatimes.com/april-16-2011/first-meeting-of-lokpal-bill-drafting-panel/slideshow/7998886.cms
11. Baba Ramdev's competitive fast, Arnab Goswami
    https://www.youtube.com/watch?v=a75QihJg91Y
    Published by Times Now, 4 May 2011.
12. 'No One Will Support Ramdev if He Goes on a Fast', PTI, Daily Bhaskar, 16 May 2011.
    http://daily.bhaskar.com/news/NAT-TOP-no-one-would-come-to-ramdevs-aid-if-he-goes-on-fast-says-digvijay-2108340.html
13. 'Baba Ramdev to Do Hazare, to Launch "Satyagraha" in Delhi',

Sources

PTI, 4 May 2011.
http://www.hindustantimes.com/mumbai/baba-ramdev-to-do-hazare-to-launch-satyagraha-in-delhi/story-ay86bIyrAkCPaHcREfkxMN.html

14. Ramdev launches anti-corruption movement. Part 1 (Ramdev responds to Digvijay Singh's allegations saying everyone who leads a movement against injustice faces charges).
https://www.youtube.com/watch?v=3PDGTnFhd-Q

15. 'Four Ministers Woo Ramdev, but He Won't Call Off Fast', *Hindustan Times*, 1 June 2011.
http://www.hindustantimes.com/delhi-news/four-ministers-woo-ramdev-but-he-won-t-call-off-fast/story-wrhtPNS5IXiAPSTo01DrQO_amp.html

16. Government's red carpet for Baba Ramdev (Ramdev received by four senior ministers at Delhi airport).
https://www.youtube.com/watch?v=4fN4 MBNbtD4
Published by Times Now, 1 June 2011.

17. 'Baba Ramdev Meets with Ministers at Claridges Hotel', NDTV, 3 June 2011.
http://www.ndtv.com/india-news/baba-ramdev-meets-with-ministers-at-claridges-hotel-457476

18. Has the government failed to handle Baba Ramdev's campaign? (NDTV reports on break down of talks between Ramdev and government after four hours of talks.)
https://www.youtube.com/watch?v=Jk9giBbv81A
Published by NDTV, 3 June 2011.

19. 'Baba Ramdev Accused of Land Grabbing'
https://www.youtube.com/watch?v=eL_LNactsIU
Published by NewsX, 4 June 2011.

20. 'Baba Ramdev, Kapil Sibal Spar over Disclosure of Letter of Understanding', ITGD Bureau, New Delhi, 4 June 2011.
http://indiatoday.intoday.in/story/baba-ramdev-kapil-sibal-spar-over-disclosure-of-letter-of-understanding/1/140405.html

21. Kapil Sibal explains the government standpoint about stand-off with Ramdev

Sources

   https://www.youtube.com/watch?v=u6DMu5v OQ58
   Published by TV9 Kannada, 5 June 2011.
22. 'Midnight Police Swoop on Baba Ramdev Ends Protests', Times News Network, 5 June 2011.
   http://timesofindia.indiatimes.com/india/Midnight-police-swoop-on-Baba-Ramdev-ends-protest/articleshow/8730121.cms
23. Police action against Ramdev's movement at Ramlila Maidan, teargas used
   https://www.youtube.com/watch?v=xPvr5YHtriI
   Published by India TV, 4 June 2011.
24. Baba Ramdev's protest in Delhi
   https://www.youtube.com/watch?v=ogD-ajd9ZfY&t=2s
   Published by News Hour India, 4 June 2011.
25. Ramdev fleeing Ramlila Maidan dressed as a woman after police action in Delhi
   https://www.youtube.com/watch?v=fVVfyUz D0XI&t=5s
   Published by CNN-News 18 7 June 2011.
26. Ramdev seen holding saffron bag, supposedly containing spare clothes given to him by the Delhi Police, Star News, 7 June 2011.
   https://www.youtube.com/watch?v=Ccx9vLaD5bo
27. Ramdev says government plans to kill me
   https://www.youtube.com/watch?v=FafssJ_fT_A
   Published by News Hour India, 5 June 2011.
28. Ramdev joins hands with Anna Hazare
   https://www.youtube.com/watch?v=IAq6 ZCKVLaA
   Published by Tv9 Gujarat, 8 April 2011.
29. 'The Rise of Baba Ramdev', Nikita Garia, *Wall Street Journal*, 1 June 2011.
   https://blogs.wsj.com/indiarealtime/2011/06/01/the-rise-of-baba-ramdev/
30. 'Baba Ramdev: The Karma Yogi', P.R. Ramesh, *Open* magazine, 30 September 2016.
   http://www.openthemagazine.com/article/cover-story/baba-ramdev-the-karma-yogi

31. 'ED Books Baba Ramdev, His Trusts for FEMA Violations', Headlines Today Bureau, *India Today*, 2 September 2011.
   http://indiatoday.intoday.in/story/ed-finds-fema-violations-by-trusts-of-baba-ramdev/1/149667.html
32. Swami Ramdev on Guru Shankar Dev issue on India TV https://www.youtube.com/watch?v=Ssl6gyXSOUk
   Published by BSNeyasMediaNews, 13 October 2013.
33. 'How Ramdev's Assets Are Being Probed', NDTV, 28 June 2011.
   http://www.ndtv.com/delhi-news/how-ramdevs-assets-are-being-probed-459735

Chapter 21: The Old Mentor Re-enters

Interviews with:
Acharya Karamveer, Vipin Pradhan, Surakshit Goswami and Tarun Kumar.

1. 'Remarks against Buddhism: HC Notice to Ramdev', *Outlook* magazine, 13 July 2011.
   http://www.outlookindia.com/newswire/story/remarks-against-buddhism-hc-notice-to-ramdev/727657
2. ED Books Baba Ramdev, His Trusts for FEMA Violation
   http://indiatoday.intoday.in/story/ed-finds-fema-violations-by-trusts-of-baba-ramdev/1/149667.html
3. 'Fake Documents Case: CBI Arrests Ramdev Aide Balkrishna', PTI, *Hindu*, 20 July 2012.
   http://www.thehindu.com/news/national/fake-documents-case-cbi-arrests-ramdevs-aide-balkrishna/article3661980.ece
4. Ramdev and Balkrishna respond to the Congress's tax evasion, land grabbing and money laundering charges, declare assets to media in press conference.
   a) https://www.youtube.com/watch?v=hIX2ueNkxlA (Part 1)
   b) https://www.youtube.com/watch?v=FK1x0i5f2uQ (Part 2)
   c) https://www.youtube.com/watch?v=0g8NjyVimXM (Part 3)
   Published by Azad Vichar, 9 June 2011.

Sources

5. Digvijay Singh accuses Ramdev of 'thugging' Shankar Dev and Karamveer, CNN-IBN, 4 June 2011.
   https://www.youtube.com/watch?v=QA094gy E3gU
6. 'Baba Black Sheep and the Golden Fleece', Manoj Rawat, *Tehelka*, 18 June 2011. http://archive.tehelka.com/story_main49.asp?filename=Ne180611Coverstory2.asp
7. CBI arrests Ramdev aide Balkrishna in fake passport case
   https://www.youtube.com/watch?v=Z2Jyr3iaw2M
   Published by ABP News, 20 July 2012.
8. Balkrishna's passport crisis
   https://www.youtube.com/watch?v=dDZVnslpRb0
   Published by Times Now, 4 August 2011.
   a) The Noida Yoga camp with Karamveer sharing the stage, 29 October 2011.
      https://www.youtube.com/watch?v=CXp91UncN1w
   b) The Noida Yoga camp with Karamveer sharing the stage, 29 October 2011.
      https://www.youtube.com/watch?v=CXp91UncN1w&t=64s
   c) https://www.youtube.com/watch?v=sI8OeprJgaM
9. 'Ramdev Spreading Nepotism: Baba Karamveer', Webindia, 12 April 2011.
   http://news.webindia123.com/news/articles/India/20110413/1728794.html

Chapter 22: The CEO

Interviews with:
S.K. Patra, Anand Shah, Abneesh Roy and Gunendar Kapur.

External Sources
1. 'Juicy Returns', Kakoly Chatterjee, *Business Today*, 20 March 2011.
   http://www.businesstoday.in/magazine/features/mega-food-parks-are-eliminating-middlemen-in-farm-to-retail-chain/story/13612.html
2. 'Tough Road ahead for Ramdev's Companies', Shishir Prashant, Rediff, 27 July 2011.

Sources

http://www.rediff.com/business/slide-show/slide-show-1-tough-road-ahead-for-ramdev-companies/20110727.htm#3

3. 'CBI, I-T to Probe Turnover of Baba Ramdev's Firms', Headlines Today Bureau, *India Today*, 7 June 2011.
http://indiatoday.intoday.in/story/baba-ramdev-firms-under-cbi-i-t-scanner/1/140628.html
4. 'Ramdev's Close Aide Balkrishna Arrested', Headlines Today, *India Today*, 20 July 2012.
http://indiatoday.intoday.in/video/baba-ramdev-balkrishna-arrested-fake-passport-case/1/209391.html
5. 'Acharya Balkrishna Appeared Court in Fake Passport Case', Jagran, 2 December 2016.
http://www.jagran.com/uttarakhand/dehradun-city-acharya-balkrishna-appeared-court-in-fake-passport-case-15136237.html
6. 'The Rise and Fall of Balkrishna', Shishir Prashant, *Business Standard*, 30 July 2011.
http://www.business-standard.com/article/beyond-business/the-rise-and-fall-of-balkrishna-111073000065_1.html
7. 'Ramdev Trusts Slapped with Demand Notice for Alleged Tax Evasion',
PTI, *Hindu*, 11 November 2012.
http://www.thehindu.com/news/national/ramdev-trusts-slapped-with-demand-notice-for-alleged-tax-evasion/article4087599.ece
8. Baba Ramdev refutes forex violation
https://www.youtube.com/watch?v=qgE1OU7My_k
Published by Times Now, 5 September 2011.
9. Ramdev accuses Congress of using its dirty tricks department to implicate him in sex, drugs and murder racket on Times Now
https://www.youtube.com/watch?v=Tqf5QbFOXuM
Published by Times Now, 14 October 2013.
10. 'How to Apply Online for Patanjali Distributorship, Mega Store or Clinic in India', Nidhi, India Study Channel, 6 April 2016.
http://www.indiastudychannel.com/resources/169242-How-to-

apply-online-for-Patanjali-distributorship-mega-store-or-clinic-in-India.aspx

11. Keith Woodford, *Devil in the Milk* (Chelsea Green Publishing, 2009).
    http://www.chelseagreen.com/devil-in-the-milk
12. 'The Devil in the Milk', Michael Schmidt, The Bovine Press, 20 March 2009.
    https://thebovine.wordpress.com/2009/03/20/the-devil-in-the-milk-dr-thomas-cowan-on-how-a2-milk-is-the-answer-to-the-mystery-of-why-even-raw-milk-sometimes-does-not-seem-to-be-enough-of-an-improvement-over-store-bought/A1-A2 protien
13. 'The Yoga Guru Turned Company Boss', Yogita Limaye, BBC News, 21 December 2015.
    http://www.bbc.com/news/business-35097567
14. 'A Retail Shocker from Haridwar: The Patanjali Story', Athira Nair, Your Story, 25 March 2016.
    https://yourstory.com/2016/03/patanjali-story/
15. 'Ramdev Turns His Ayurveda Enterprise into FMCG Empire', Namrata Acharya, *Business Standard*, 28 June 2015.
    http://www.business-standard.com/article/companies/ramdev-turns-his-ayurved-enterprise-into-an-fmcg-empire-115062800143_1.html

Chapter 23: The Brother

1. 'Baba Ramdev's Brother Injures Two in Car Crash', NDTV, 17 June 2010.
   http://www.ndtv.com/cities/baba-ramdevs-brother-injures-two-in-car-crash-421099
2. 'HC Stays Arrest of Ramdev's Brother Ram Bharat', *DNA*, 28 October 2013.
   http://www.dnaindia.com/india/report-hc-stays-arrest-of-ramdev-s-brother-ram-bharat-1910292
3. 'Patanjali Shootout: Ramdev's Brother Jailed for 14 days', Kautilya

Sources

Singh and Sheo A. Jaiswali, *Times of India*, 29 May 2015.
http://timesofindia.indiatimes.com/city/dehradun/Patanjali-food-park-shootout-Ramdevs-brother-jailed-for-14-days/articleshow/47461158.cms

4. 'Non-bailable Warrant Issued against Baba Ramdev's Brother', *Daily Pioneer*, 29 October 2013.
http://www.dailypioneer.com/state-editions/dehradun/non-bailable-warrant-issued-against-baba-ramdevs-brother.html

5. 'Cops Forced FIR against Ramdev's Brother', Sunil Kumar, *Daily Pioneer*, 29 October 2013.
http://www.dailypioneer.com/todays-newspaper/cops-forced-fir-against-ramdevs-brother-suer.html

6. 'Patanjali Shootout: Ramdev Seen in Footage, Brother Accused of Instigating Attack', Dainik Bhaskar News Network, 30 May 2015.
http://daily.bhaskar.com/news/NAT-TOP-patanjali-food-park-shootout-baba-ramdev-in-cctv-footage-brother-ram-bharat-inst-5008193-PHO.html

7. 'CCTV Footage Shows Ramdev's Brother Instigating Attack', Shalini Narayan, *Indian Express*, 30 May 2015.
http://indianexpress.com/article/india/india-others/cctv-footage-shows-ramdevs-brother-instigating-attack-police/

8. 'Illegal Weapons: Fresh Notice to Ramdev Park for Details on Guards', Shalini Narayan, *Indian Express*, 1 June 2015.
http://indianexpress.com/article/india/india-others/illegal-weapons-fresh-notice-to-ramdevs-park-for-details-on-guards/

9. Ram Bharat Arrested in Patanjali Clash – Interview of SSP Sweety Aggrawal
https://www.youtube.com/watch?v=KMc4xWVF72c
Published by Pradesh 19 English, 27 May 2015.

10. Patanjali shootout: Ramdev seen in CCTV footage
https://www.youtube.com/watch?v=ODzVFNhLP_M
Published by News 24, 29 May 2015.

11. 'One Killed in Haridwar Patanjali Food Park, Ramdev's Brother Arrested', Kavita Upadhyay, *Hindu*, 27 May 2015.

Sources

      http://www.thehindu.com/news/national/other-states/one-killed-four-injured-in-a-clash-in-ramdevs-patanjali-food-park-in-haridwar/article7251694.ece

12. 'Ramdev Food Park Clash: Twist in Probe, Cops Say Union Members', Shalini Narayan, *Indian Express*, 9 June 2015.
    http://indianexpress.com/article/india/india-others/ramdev-food-park-clash-twist-in-probe-cops-say-union-members-attacked-first/

Chapter 24: Patanjali Ayurveda Limited

1. 'Baba Ramdev's Patanjali Turnover Is a Staggering Rs 10,561 Crores',
   Financial Express, 4 May 2017.
   http://www.financialexpress.com/industry/baba-ramdevs-patanjali-turnover-is-a-staggering-rs-10561-crore-in-fy17-100-rise-in-profits/653754/
2. 'Patanjali's Turnover for Financial Year 2016 is Rs 10,561 Crores', Scroll, 4 May 2017.
   https://scroll.in/latest/836561/patanjalis-turnover-for-financial-year-2016-2017-is-rs-10561-crore-says-ramdev
3. 'Patanjali Eyes Two-Fold Rise in Revenue at Rs 20,000 Crores', Sounak Mitra, *Mint*, 4 May 2017.
   http://www.livemint.com/Industry/cjCMZnD0eGkYOMjayFuUVN/Patanjali-eyes-2fold-rise-in-revenue-at-Rs-20000-crore-in.html
4. 'Bend It Like Baba', *Economist*, 29 April 2017.
   http://www.economist.com/news/business/21721440-baba-ramdev-has-spearheaded-billion-dollar-juggernaut-indias-patanjali-takes-western
5. I don't wait for permissions, says Ramdev at National Building Meet, New Delhi
   https://www.youtube.com/watch?v=g0XGxZmuySw (@4.20s into video)
   Published by Bharat Swabhiman, 4 March 2017.

Sources

6. Black money conversation between Ramdev and Chand Nath
   https://www.youtube.com/watch?v=AOKhG8sxWW4
   Published by Funny Nation, 13 November 2016.
7. Ramdev caught on camera discussing money with BJP leader
   https://www.youtube.com/watch?v=7EV36w2cNu4
   Published by Aaj Tak, 18 April 2014.
8. 'Ramdev's Patanjali Launches Noodles', PTI, *Hindu*, 16 November 2015.
   http://www.thehindu.com/business/ramdevs-patanjali-launches-noodles/article7884161.ece
9. Ramdev launches atta noodles
   https://www.youtube.com/watch?v=KOzrjCHFy3Q
10. 'Noodles Launched by Ramdev Have No Approval', Abantika Ghosh, *Indian Express*, 18 November 2015.
    http://indianexpress.com/article/india/india-news-india/noodles-launched-by-ramdev-have-no-approval-says-fssai/
11. 'No Licence for Noodles: FSSAI Slaps Showcause on Patanjali', Utkarsh Anand, Abantika Ghosh, *Indian Express*, 21 November 2015.
    http://indianexpress.com/article/india/india-news-india/no-licence-for-noodles-fssai-slaps-showcause-on-patanjali/
12. Open to scrutiny on Patanjali noodles from any agency, says Ramdev
    http://www.news18.com/videos/india/open-to-scrutiny-on-patanjali-noodles-from-any-agency-says-ramdev-1166559.html
    Published by News18, 20 November 2015.
13. 'Patanjali, Food Operators Don't Need Approval from FSSAI', Aditi Tandon, Tribune, 19 November 2015.
    http://www.tribuneindia.com/news/nation/patanjali-other-food-operators-don-t-need-approval-from-fssai/160093.html
14. 'Worms Found in Baba Ramdev's Patanjali Noodles', Ajay Kumar, *India Today*, 7 December 2015.
    http://indiatoday.intoday.in/story/worms-found-in-patanjali-noodles/1/540075.html
15. 'Baba Ramdev Alleges MNCs of Conspiring against Patanjali',

Sources

DNA, 1 February 2016.
http://www.dnaindia.com/money/report-baba-ramdev-alleges-mncs-of-conspiring-against-patanjali-2172871

16. Ramdev sees conspiracy, says MNCs are scared of Patanjali products
    https://www.youtube.com/watch?v=g6V82Ok_IYU
    Published by India TV, 1 February 2016.
17. Ramdev's six products fail government test
    https://www.youtube.com/watch?v=amwlG3kDKrU&t=20s
    Published by ABP News, 25 September 2012.
18. 'Baba Ramdev's Patanjali Ayurveda Fined Rs 11 Lakhs for Misleading Advertisements', PTI, *Mint*, 15 December 2016.
    http://www.livemint.com/Consumer/AJZSR4R9Oipf4SCj ZBDRRI/Baba-Ramdevs-Patanjali-Ayurved-fined-Rs11-lakh-for-misleadi.html?gclid=CN_zv8DJpdQCFY0XaAodHh0Opw
19. 'Ghee, Cream Under Scrutiny: Haryana FDA Finds some Brands "Substandard"', Deepak Patel, *Indian Express*, 18 April 2017.
    http://indianexpress.com/article/business/companies/haryana-fda-finds-certain-items-of-milk-brands-substandard-4617242/
20. 'Ramdev's Patanjali Fined Rs 11 lakh for Putting Up Misleading Advertisements', PTI, *Indian Express*, 15 December 2017.
    http://indianexpress.com/article/india/ramdevs-patanjali-fined-rs-11-lakh-for-putting-up-misleading-advertisements-4427776/
21. 'Patanjali Defends Amla Juice, Says It's a Medicinal Product', Sounak Mitra, *Mint*, 25 April 2017.
    http://www.livemint.com/Companies/KWfFBljtKZlRQ Znm9fVbaP/Patanjali-defends-amla-juice-says-its-a-medicinal-product.html
22. 'Defence CSD Suspends Sale of Patanjali's Amla Juice', Sagar Malviya, *Economic Times*, 24 April 2017.
    http://economictimes.indiatimes.com/industry/cons-products/food/defences-csd-suspends-sale-of-patanjalis-amla-juice/articleshow/58332920.cms
23. 'Colgate to Battle Patanjali Dant Kanti with Herbal Toothpaste Vedshakti',

Sagar Malviya and Neha Tyagi, *Economic Times*, 1 August 2016.
http://economictimes.indiatimes.com/industry/cons-products/fmcg/colgate-to-battle-patanjalis-dant-kanti-with-herbal-toothpaste-vedshakti/articleshow/53482249.cms
24. 'Hindustan Unilever Indulekha Hair Oil Brand', Reghu Balakrishnan, *Mint*, 18 December 2015.
http://www.livemint.com/Companies/HGJpUwbffqvA2Jmwng5MfN/Hindustan-Unilever-buys-Indulekha-hair-oil-brand.html
25. Dabur India. Report, *Business Standard*, 4 January 2016.
http://bsmedia.business-standard.com/_media/bs/data/market-reports/equity-brokertips/2016-01/14518980490.14493300.pdf
26. 'After Patanjali, Existing FMCG Players may face Challenge from Sri Sri Ravi Shankar's Sri Sri Ayurveda', Jwalit Vyas, *Economic Times*, 17 March 2017.
http://economictimes.indiatimes.com/industry/cons-products/fmcg/after-patanjali-existing-fmcg-players-may-face-challenge-from-sri-sri-ravi-shankars-sri-sri-ayurveda/articleshow/51433950.cms
27. http://isha.sadhguru.org/isha-store/

Chapter 25: Conclusion

1. 'Balkrishna Claims to have Discovered the Sanjeevani Buti', Webindia
http://news.webindia123.com/news/articles/India/20090301/1188491.html
2. 'Reuters Investigation in Ramdev's Politics', Rahul Bhatia and Tom Lasseter, Reuters, 23 May 2017.
http://www.reuters.com/investigates/special-report/india-modi-ramdev/
3. 'How True Is Baba Ramdev's Theory of All Conspiracies?' Akash Deep Ashok, *India Today*, 22 October 2013.
http://indiatoday.intoday.in/story/baba-ramdev-conspiracies-asaram-bapu-rambharat-kidnapping-charges/1/317443.html

Acknowledgements

For a life extraordinarily lived, for all those things that made telling his story such an adventure, I thank Baba Ramdev.

I am very grateful to the cast of characters – not all of them made it to the book – for helping me with information, insight and advice and trusting me with their often very personal stories and memories.

Thank you to all the chroniclers – the dogged journalists and citizen journalists who have followed, questioned, analysed, written, reported and recorded the life and times of Baba Ramdev in such incredible detail. This book relies on and draws deeply from all your amazing work.

Thank you Parth Mehrotra, my wonderful editor, who helped battle through mountains of research to bring the book to life. Thank you Chiki Sarkar, at Juggernaut, for all the hand-holding when this project seemed a little daunting in its scope!

I'm very grateful to my family and friends who have steadfastly encouraged, listened, supported and offered advice through the reporting and writing of the book.

Finally, a thank you to two amazing editors I've had the honour of working with, Mitra Kalita and Raju Narisetti, whose encouragement and support have played an important role in my pursuit of dispassionate, balanced, explanatory journalism in India.

A Note on the Author

Priyanka Pathak-Narain graduated from Columbia Journalism School in 2007, and wrote about the business of religion at *Mint* between 2007 and 2013. She won the CNN Young Journalist Award for her coverage of the Setusamudram channel project in 2007. A contributing writer for *Dharavi: The City Within*, she occasionally writes for the *New York Times* and the Condé Nast Group.

Click the QR Code with a QR scanner app
or type the link into the Internet browser
on your phone to download the app.

SCAN TO READ THIS BOOK ON YOUR PHONE

www.juggernaut.in

DOWNLOAD THE APP

www.juggernaut.in

For our complete catalogue, visit www.juggernaut.in
To submit your book, send a synopsis and two
sample chapters to books@juggernaut.in
For all other queries, write to contact@juggernaut.in